TECHNICAL REPORT

Year of the Air Force Family

2009 Survey of Active-Duty Spouses

Laura L. Miller, Sarah O. Meadows,
Lawrence M. Hanser, Stephanie L. Taylor

Prepared for the United States Air Force

PROJECT AIR FORCE

The research described in this report was sponsored by the United States Air Force under Contract FA7014-06-C-0001. Further information may be obtained from the Strategic Planning Division, Directorate of Plans, Hq USAF.

Library of Congress Cataloging-in-Publication Data

Year of the Air Force family : 2009 survey of active-duty spouses / Laura L. Miller ... [et al.].
   p. cm.
 Includes bibliographical references.
 ISBN 978-0-8330-5096-0 (pbk. : alk. paper)
 1. Air Force spouses—Services for—United States. 2. Air Force spouses—United States—Attitudes—Statistics.
3. Families of military personnel—Services for—United States—Statistics. I. Miller, Laura L., 1967-

UG633.Y43 2011
358.4'1120973090511—dc22

                                                           2011002668

The RAND Corporation is a nonprofit institution that helps improve policy and decisionmaking through research and analysis. RAND's publications do not necessarily reflect the opinions of its research clients and sponsors.

RAND® is a registered trademark.

Published 2011 by the RAND Corporation
1776 Main Street, P.O. Box 2138, Santa Monica, CA 90407-2138
1200 South Hayes Street, Arlington, VA 22202-5050
4570 Fifth Avenue, Suite 600, Pittsburgh, PA 15213-2665
RAND URL: http://www.rand.org/
To order RAND documents or to obtain additional information, contact
Distribution Services: Telephone: (310) 451-7002;
Fax: (310) 451-6915; Email: order@rand.org

Preface

This report conveys the results of a telephone survey administered in summer 2009 to a random stratified sample of 802 spouses of active-duty airmen. The survey focused on specific problems families might face and factors associated with them, family use of recreational services, and attitudes about Air Force leadership and Air Force life. These findings informed organizational efforts during the 2009–2010 Year of the Air Force Family and beyond.

The research described in this report was conducted by RAND Project AIR FORCE within its Manpower, Personnel, and Training Program as part of a fiscal year 2009 study, "Air Force Culture." The Deputy Chief of Staff for Manpower and Personnel, Headquarters U.S. Air Force and its Airman and Family Services Branch sponsored the study. This report should be of interest to Air Force leadership, Air Force families themselves, as well as professionals and semiprofessionals who work both formally and informally with Air Force families.

RAND Project AIR FORCE

RAND Project AIR FORCE (PAF), a division of the RAND Corporation, is the U.S. Air Force's federally funded research and development center for studies and analyses. PAF provides the Air Force with independent analyses of policy alternatives affecting the development, employment, combat readiness, and support of current and future aerospace forces. Research is conducted in four programs: Force Modernization and Employment; Manpower, Personnel, and Training; Resource Management; and Strategy and Doctrine.

Additional information about PAF is available on our website:
http://www.rand.org/paf/

Contents

APPENDIXES

Figures

Tables

Summary

Air Force leaders are concerned about the well-being of Air Force families, the types and causes of problems they face, and whether Air Force support programs successfully assist families with these problems. Leaders are also interested in families' perceptions of Air Force leadership and satisfaction with Air Force life. To provide the Air Force with insights on a subset of problems our sponsor identified as their highest priority, we conducted a telephone survey of a representative sample of 802 military and civilian spouses of active-duty officers and enlisted airmen in July and August 2009.

The survey focused primarily on child-related, financial, and employment problems that families had experienced in the past year. We analyzed the data to produce overall Air Force spouse results and to identify any significant differences between the particular subgroups of greatest interest to our research sponsor, comparing spouses of officers with spouses of enlisted airmen, dual-military couples with civilian spouses, families residing on and off base, and families having minor children at home with those that did not. The following are our overall results:

- Thirty-seven percent of all respondents reported at least one child-related problem. Difficulties finding child care and child emotional and behavioral problems were most common examples.
- Among families with children and at least one parent deployed recently, 52 percent reported that the deployment worsened their child-related problems, and few reported that the problems improved.
- Of the 26 percent of spouses reporting at least one financial problem, an inability to save money was the most common, cited by 24 percent of respondents.
- Among respondents who indicated at least one financial problem and a recent deployment, 35 percent reported that financial problems improved, 36 percent reported that they did not change, and the remaining 29 percent that they worsened during deployments.
- Thirty-seven percent of all respondents reported spousal employment problems, which most frequently involved difficulty being able to work a preferred schedule or number of hours and difficulty finding a job, especially one appropriate to the respondent's education, abilities, and interests.
- For spouses who had had at least one employment problem and a recent deployment, 44 percent reported that employment problems worsened during deployment, while 9 percent said their situation had improved. Forty-eight percent reported that deployment had no effect on their employment issues.

The survey also asked spouses who reported problems whether they associated particular factors with the problems. Spouses commonly associated child-related problems with a recent move or permanent change of station (PCS), their work schedule, and/or the hours Air Force child care is available. Ten percent or more of spouses associated the problems relating to their children with the distance from Air Force activities for children, distance from Air Force day care, and/or the limitations of Air Force programs. The factors most commonly associated with financial problems were costs of raising children, the spouse's employment status, and a recent move or PCS. Notably, 30 percent of those with financial problems reported associated them with a lack of information about Air Force financial education programs, while 34 percent said that lack of information about spousal employment assistance programs was related to their employment problems. The factors most commonly associated with spousal employment problems were difficulties finding a job that paid enough to cover the costs of child care, a recent PCS, and finding child care that matched the parent's working hours. Around 30 percent of respondents with employment problems also linked their employment problems to a lack of information about Air Force employment assistance programs, inconvenient access to the programs, and/or inability of the programs to address the specific problems.

Our subgroup analyses showed that the differences between dual-military and civilian spouses were more prevalent across the survey items than were the differences between the other subgroups (officer and enlisted; residence on or off base; and between parents and non-parents for issues not related to children). Compared to civilian spouses, dual-military parents were more likely to report problems finding child care while they worked or attended school and were more likely to associate their child-related problems with their work schedule and the hours Air Force child care is available. Dual-military spouses who had experienced a recent deployment were much more likely than their civilian peers to report that deployments did not affect their employment-related problems and were more likely to have attended deployment briefings.

Civilian spouses were more likely than dual-military spouses to report financial problems and were more likely to associate their employment status with them. Civilian spouses were also more likely to experience each of the employment-related problems on our survey or to have any employment problems at all. Deployments were more likely to negatively affect the employment status of civilian spouses than of dual-military spouses. Civilians were significantly more likely than their dual-military counterparts to associate five of six possible factors with employment problems.

These subgroups also differed in their preferred means of communication about Air Force programs and services: Dual-military spouses were more likely to prefer emails and posters or flyers on base, while civilians were more likely to prefer direct mailings and Air Force newspapers and newsletters.

Family participation in leisure activities can help relieve stress and anxiety, build skills and confidence, strengthen family bonds, and facilitate friendships with other families. Nearly every respondent participated in at least one of the ten leisure activities listed in our survey. Use of the local gym or fitness center was the most common activity (about 85 percent), followed by bowling (about 70 percent) and outdoor recreational activities (about 65 percent). Many families rely on Air Force programs and facilities to meet their leisure needs either wholly or partially. Of the roughly one-third of families who participate in arts and crafts with other people, however, more than half engage in these activities entirely off base.

In spite of noted child, financial, employment problems and the effects of deployments and PCSing, over 90 percent of all spouses were satisfied with their lives and their family's well-being, and 84 percent were satisfied with Air Force family life. The majority of spouses (at least 60 percent) agreed that their spouse's supervisor, unit leader, and senior Air Force leadership cared about Air Force family well-being. Eighty-three percent indicated that their families were likely to remain in the Air Force for another tour of duty. Despite the significantly different experiences that civilian and dual-military spouses reported in terms of problems and associated factors, both groups evaluated their life satisfaction, opinion of Air Force leadership, and organizational commitment the same way.

The Air Force has a number of options to improve support for Air Force families:

- Expand assistance with the PCS transition to minimize disruptions to spousal employment, family finances, and child well-being.
- Increase the availability, both in terms of time and slots, of child care.
- Expand and better publicize youth activities available after school or on weekends.
- Support greater on-base recreational programming for arts, crafts, and hobbies popular with spouses and their families.
- Deepen support to families throughout the deployment cycle, particularly with regard to the needs of children and the employment of spouses remaining at home.
- Better promote financial and employment assistance programs.
- Improve employment opportunities for military spouses through partnerships with national companies and Air Force contractors.
- Use spouses' preferred means of communication, including emails, websites, and newsletters and newspapers, to convey information about outreach efforts and publicize new or modified programs and policies.
- Finally, the Air Force's ability to support families would be enhanced if it centrally collected direct contact information for spouses.

Acknowledgments

We would like to thank Eliza Nesmith and Gretchen H. Shannon of the Air Force's Airman and Family Services Branch for their thoughtful and informative guidance throughout the research process. They and their staff, particularly Leslie Joseph and Anne-Marie Wallace, provided valuable input on the design of the survey instrument to help ensure that the results would meet the needs of Air Force leadership.

Our RAND colleague, Nelson Lim, provided advice that informed our sample design, and we are grateful for his contributions. Robert Magaw and Lisa Gowing at Abt SRBI led an impressive and well-documented survey administration effort.

By reviewing our draft manuscript, RAND colleagues Marc Elliot and Sandra Berry helped us significantly improve the description of our survey methods. Morten Ender of the United States Military Academy at West Point and Mady Segal, Professor Emerita at the University of Maryland at College Park, also reviewed the document, leading us to make important clarifications, conduct some additional analyses, and better connect our findings to the larger body of research on military personnel and their families. Phyllis Gilmore's expert editing improved our writing and data presentation.

Abbreviations

AFPC   Air Force Personnel Center

AAPOR   American Association of Public Opinion Research

CHA   Craft and Hobby Association

CONUS   continental United States (excludes Alaska and Hawaii)

DMDC   Defense Manpower Data Center

EFMP   Exceptional Family Member Program

NCO   noncommissioned officer

OCONUS   outside the continental United States

PAF   Project AIR FORCE

PCS   permanent change of station

CHAPTER ONE

Introduction

To Inform the Year of the Air Force Family

The Secretary of the Air Force and the Air Force Chief of Staff designated July 2009 to July 2010 as the Year of the Air Force Family, pledging to focus on "hardships and needs, what we might do to make Air Force life more compatible with family life, and how we can build a greater sense of community across our force" (Donley, 2009). These senior leaders identified housing, children's education, medical care, and child care as the four basic needs of Air Force families (Donley, 2009). Furthermore, in July 2010, the Chief of Staff, General Norton A. Schwartz, named the development of and care for airmen and their families as one of his five priorities for the future.

To support Air Force leaders' efforts to understand the challenges Air Force families are facing and the policy revisions that might help meet these challenges, RAND Project AIR FORCE (PAF) designed and analyzed a survey of spouses of active-duty U.S. Air Force personnel. The study fell under the direction of the Airman and Family Services Branch, which helped determine the survey population and survey domains.[1] The branch manages a vast array of support services for both single and married airmen, many of which are coordinated through the Airman and Family Readiness Centers (formerly known as Family Support Centers) on Air Force bases.

The study sponsors asked PAF to design an instrument that would ask spouses about problems they might be having related to relocation; family finances; deployment experiences; their own education and employment; and child care, education, and well-being. Although the research literature on military families contains very few studies devoted to Air Force families in particular, these categories have been commonly explored as among the challenges of military life (e.g., Booth, Segal, and Bell, 2007; Burrell et al. 2006; Cooke and Speirs, 2005; Drummet, Coleman, and Cable, 2004; Lim, Golinelli, and Cho, 2007; Martin, Rosen, and Sparacino, 2000; McClure, 1999; Segal, 1986).

The research sponsors asked us not to treat each realm as a separate, stand-alone category but to treat them all as factors that may interact and influence one another. To accomplish this, we organized the survey to ask spouses, first, whether they had encountered any of the problems we categorized as being related to their finances, employment, or children. Then, we asked those who had encountered problems in any of these areas about possible associated factors, such as relocations and deployments. We limited associated factors to those the Air Force

---

[1] In terms of survey domains, child care and spousal employment assistance programs are overseen by the Airman and Family Services Branch, but airman and dependent medical care is the responsibility of the Air Force Surgeon General.

Office of Services had programs and services designed to address, so the list does not include all possible related factors (e.g., personal illness).

Additional questions measured other items of interest. The Air Force devotes a great deal of resources toward recreational programs and facilities and so also asked us to capture the usage of these services on base, off base, or both. Finally, the Air Force asked us to include some items that focused on how spouses perceived their family's overall well-being, how satisfied they were with Air Force life, and the opinions they had about Air Force leaders.

It is important to acknowledge what this survey was not designed to do. It does not provide an overall evaluation of the strengths and weaknesses of Air Force family programs. Neither does it attempt to assess all possible problems Air Force families might be facing. It also does not ask Air Force families to propose the course of action the Air Force should take to help them resolve these problems, or whether they even expect the Air Force to do so. And finally, the survey was not designed to capture the perspectives of active-duty airmen themselves.

Organization of This Report

The remainder of the report describes the survey effort, reports the findings, and offers policy options for the Air Force to explore.

Chapter Two will interest those who wish to learn about the survey methods and sample: who was selected for participation in the study and why, how the survey was administered, and what the demographic characteristics of the weighted sample are.

Chapter Three reports the results of the survey items on the financial, spousal employment and child-related problems, as well as some of the possible associated factors.

Chapter Four conveys information about the level of use of specific Air Force services and programs related to deployment and recreation. It also provides spouses' assessments of overall levels of family well-being, satisfaction with Air Force life, and opinions about Air Force leaders.

Chapter Five offers recommendations for additional inquiries during the Year of the Air Force Family and policy options that Manpower and Personnel, Headquarters U.S. Air Force, should consider.

The survey instrument appears in Appendix A; Appendix B provides details about the calculation of sample response rates; and Appendix C provides some technical details on the construction of the sample weights.

CHAPTER TWO

Sample and Methods

The survey was designed to address specific types of problems Air Force families might face that existing Air Force programs already address; to discover whether and how the problems relate to particular issues that the Air Force is able to influence; to get an overall sense of how well Air Force families are doing; and to assess attitudes toward the Air Force, including its leadership, support services, and Air Force life in general, from a military spouse's perspective. As such, this survey did not include single-parent families. It was conducted via telephone in July and August 2009. The total sample consisted of 802 spouses of active-duty airmen and included spouses who are part of both dual-military and civilian-military couples. What follows is a description of how the sample was designed, how the survey was administered, the response rates, and how the sample was weighted so that the results are representative of the married, active-duty Air Force spouse population as a whole.

Sampling Design

The sample was designed to represent all married, active-duty Air Force personnel. We worked with the research sponsor to determine which demographic categories were most important and counterbalanced the desire for numerous subgroups against survey administration costs. From among several subgroups of interest, the sponsor chose two key demographics of interest: whether the spouse was married to an officer or an enlisted airman and whether the spouse was a civilian or a military member as well (regardless of service branch or component). A random stratified sample of 800 spouses was deemed sufficient to meet the goals of the sponsor while meeting survey budget constraints.

The entire population of spouses of more than 190,000 married, active-duty airmen was eligible to be selected for the survey. This population was first divided into four non-overlapping subpopulations:

1. officers married to civilians
2. officers married to other military members
3. enlisted personnel married to civilians
4. enlisted personnel married to other military members.

We drew a random sample of 805 from the first subpopulation, 805 from the second subpopulation, 1,000 from the third subpopulation, and 1,390 from the fourth subpopulation. The categories of spouses married to officers and spouses in dual-military families were oversampled relative to their actual rates of occurrence in the population because there were fewer of them in the population of married active-duty Air Force personnel.

The ordering of individuals in the sample from each subpopulation was randomized within each subpopulation. The four subpopulation samples were provided to the survey administration company as separate lists along with the minimum desired sample sizes shown in Figure 2.1.[1]

Survey Administration

At least one week before the call from a survey interviewer, the spouses in the stratified random sample received notification letters signed by the research sponsor. For these letters, we used the home mailing addresses listed in the Air Force Personnel Center (AFPC) database. In the letter, spouses were given the option of initiating the call and scheduling a convenient time to complete the interview if they wished. A total of 2,936 notification letters were mailed to spouses. Home telephone numbers listed in the Air Force personnel file, whether cell phones or landlines, were used to contact spouses to conduct the survey itself.[2] Interviewers attempted to reach spouses not only on weekdays but also in the evenings and on weekends.

Participation in the survey was voluntary and confidential. Respondents were permitted to skip any questions they did not want to answer or to end the interview early if necessary or desired. The Air Force did not receive data that could identify individual respondents.[3]

The survey was administered in July and August 2009. This timing may have presented a challenge in reaching spouses with children because many families time vacations or moves for the summer break from school.

On average, respondents completed the interview in 13 minutes, with the shortest interview at just less than seven minutes and the longest interview at just over 30 minutes. The number of questions spouses were asked varied, however. For example, those without minor children in the home were not asked questions about child-related problems and associated factors, and those who had not experienced a recent deployment were not asked deployment-related questions.

Calls to a total of 2,601 telephone numbers were attempted before the final sample of 802 was achieved. Table 2.1 shows the disposition codes for those 2,601 telephone numbers. Of those numbers dialed, 19 percent were bad numbers (i.e., disconnected, out of reach, or

---

[1]   See Appendix B for a detailed discussion of the sample's construction.

[2]   Survey access via cell phones is more expensive because the Telephone Consumer Protection Act prevents autodialing cell phones and because manual dialing is more labor intensive. We were concerned about omitting cell phones, however, because the number of adults living in households with cell phones only (known as wireless substitution) continues to rise: In 2007, 27.9 percent of adults 18–24 years old and nearly 31 percent of adults 25–29 years old fell into this category (Blumberg and Luke, 2007). Furthermore, in previous studies, wireless-only study participants responded differently from those with landlines on such issues as health-related behaviors, assessments of health status, and financial barriers to health care (Blumberg and Luke, 2007). Previous research on guard and reserve populations found that junior enlisted personnel and their spouses were particularly likely to have only cell phone numbers on file (Castaneda et al., 2008). For these reasons, we did not eliminate anyone from the sample who listed cell phone numbers for home phones, despite the expense and additional practical hurdles (e.g., respondents answering the call while driving). For more on the legal, ethical, and other issues related to conducting surveys through cell phones, see Lavrakas et al., 2007.

[3]   RAND's Institutional Review Board, the Human Subjects' Protection Committee, approved the conduct of this research.

Figure 2.1
Target Sample Stratified by Officer and Enlisted Status
and by Civilian and Dual-Military Spouse

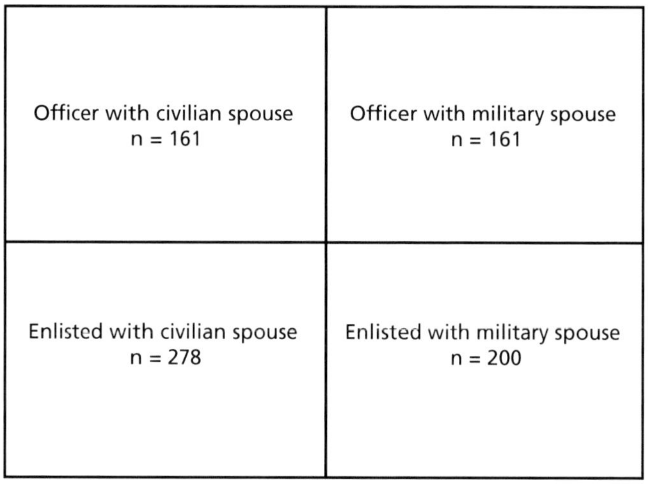

Officer with civilian spouse n = 161	Officer with military spouse n = 161
Enlisted with civilian spouse n = 278	Enlisted with military spouse n = 200

RAND *TR879-2.1*

Table 2.1
Disposition of Telephone Numbers Contacted or Attempted to Be Contacted

Disposition Status	Quantity	Proportion (percent)
Telephone numbers attempted	2,601	100
Not eligible (AAPOR Cat. 4)	494	19
Household refused to participate (AAPOR Cat. 2.1)	193	7
Participant screened out (AAPOR Cat. 1.1)	117	4
Partial interview (AAPOR Cat. 1.2)	22	1
Completed interview (AAPOR Cat. 1)	802	31
Unable to reach spouse or conduct interview prior to survey closing	973	37

wrong number).[4] Seven percent of households that were contacted refused to participate (18 cases passed the screening questions and were qualified to respond but declined to participate); 5 percent were screened out (e.g., the household did not contain an airman; the airman was not married; or the spouse was not eligible because he or she was not over the age of 18). Roughly 1 percent consisted of partial interviews that were not included in our analysis. The numbers called to achieve the 802 completed interviews comprised 31 percent of the attempted telephone numbers. For the remaining 37 percent of attempted numbers, interviewers were unable to reach and interview the spouse before the goal had been achieved.

---

[4] Counting only airmen with international telephone numbers, the percentage of bad numbers increases to 88 percent.

Using the American Association of Public Opinion Research (AAPOR) response rate definition 3, we estimate that the overall response rate was between 47 and 49 percent.[5] Using the AAPOR cooperation rate definition 3, we estimate that the cooperation rate was between 77 and 81 percent.[6]

Characteristics of the Sample

The sample of 802 was weighted to be representative of the entire population of married active-duty airmen. Weighting does not ensure that the results are completely representative. For example, approximately 17 percent of the telephone numbers dialed were disconnected or not in service. If these numbers had been disconnected as the result of financial hardship, the degree of financial hardship would be underrepresented in our results, and we have no way of knowing this for certain. For our analyses, we assumed that, after controlling for the several variables used in the weighting model, nonrespondents do not differ from respondents on any variables or characteristics that relate to the survey measures. Appendix C describes the weighting procedure we used.

Analyses were completed using survey estimation procedures to ensure appropriate estimates of standard errors (StataCorp, 2007). Table 2.2 presents demographic characteristics as represented in the weighted and unweighted samples.[7] Although we did not weight by gender, approximately 84 percent of the spouses in the weighted sample are female, which is in keeping with data for married Air Force personnel in the administrative records.[8] Approximately 20 percent of the weighted sample is in a dual-military marriage, in which at least one partner is in the active-duty Air Force and the other partner is in any branch or military component of the armed forces. About three-quarters of our sample are married to enlisted active-duty airmen. The average age of spouses was 32.4 years old, with more than one-quarter of spouses in the 25–29 age group. According to 2000 Census data, military wives are significantly younger than their civilian counterparts, at an average age of 33.2 compared to 41.9 years old (Lim, Golinelli, and Cho, 2007, p. 67). Husbands of military personnel are also younger than husbands of civilians, with an average age of 35.5 compared to 44.1 (Lim, Golinelli, and Cho, 2007, p. 66).

Residence

According to the 2000 Census, military families move further and more frequently than civilian families, and Army and Air Force wives are most likely to move to or from abroad (Lim,

---

[5]   See Appendix B for a further discussion of how we calculated response rates. According to a 2004 Pew study, comparable response rates among the civilian population were 27 percent for standard surveys and 51 percent for rigorous surveys (those that used callbacks or offered incentives for cooperation).

[6]   See Appendix B for a further discussion of how we calculated the cooperation rates. According to a 2004 Pew study, comparable cooperation rates among the civilian population were roughly 38 percent for standard surveys and 59 percent for rigorous surveys, (those that used callbacks or offered incentives for participation).

[7]   The *unweighted sample* refers to the 802 respondents to the survey. The percentages reported in this column do not take the weights into account.

[8]   Unfortunately for our purposes, the administrative records do not contain demographic details about spouses, so we cannot compare the age, race, ethnicity, education level, or employment status of those in our sample to those in the active-duty Air Force population.

Table 2.2
Characteristics of the Sample

Characteristics	Detail	Proportion of Weighted Sample (percent)	Proportion of Unweighted Sample (percent)
Gender	Female	83.7	76.1
Couple's military status	Both military	20.3	45.0
	Married to enlisted member	76.3	59.7
Spouse's age group[a]	18–24	17.2	15.4
	25–29	26.6	25.7
	30–34	18.2	20.2
	35–39	15.6	17.5
	40–44	14.6	13.5
	45–49	5.1	4.8
	50+	3.9	4.0
Residence			
On base		25.1	19.6
Off base (commute time)	Less than 30 minutes	74.1	75.0
	30 or more minutes	25.9	25.0
CONUS		94.3	94.4
With custodial child(ren) (only)	Under age 6	46.1	47.0
	Between ages 6 and 18	40.1	36.4
	Under 18	68.3	67.0
	Over 18	4.7	3.8
	With special needs	8.5	7.8
Spouse's highest educational level	Less than high school	0.7	0.4
	High school or GED	18.6	14.4
	Some college	28.0	23.9
	Associate's degree	17.3	16.2
	Bachelor's degree	23.5	25.8
	Graduate or professional degree	11.8	19.4
Spouse's student status	All spouses—full-time	10.5	8.9
	All spouses—part-time	11.8	14.8
	Civilian spouses only—full-time	11.8	11.3
	Civilian spouses only—part-time	7.0	6.7
Spouse's employment status	All spouses—full-time	42.0	49.5
	All spouses—part-time	13.9	14.8
	Civilian spouses only—full-time	32.4	31.2
	Civilian spouses only—part-time	16.5	16.5

[a] The average age of spouses in the weighted sample was 32.4; the average was 32.6 in the unweighted sample.

Golinelli, and Cho, 2007, pp. 23–24).[9] Additionally, more than 80 percent of military wives live in metropolitan areas (Lim, Golinelli, and Cho, 2007, p. 25).[10]

Ninety-four percent of the survey respondents live within the continental United States (CONUS), which includes all of the United States except Alaska and Hawaii. This overrepresentation is a known limitation of the sample: The actual CONUS representation in the population is 78 percent.[11] The imbalance is due to the particularly high amount of incomplete, incorrect, or missing home contact information for airmen living outside CONUS (OCONUS).

Most spouses live on or very near an Air Force base, which means they are not physically far from most Air Force facilities, including recreational facilities and Airman and Family Readiness Centers. One-quarter of spouses of active-duty airmen reported living on base. Of those living off base, approximately three-quarters (74 percent) live within a 30-minute drive from the base. Physical distance does not necessarily measure accessibility of base resources, however. For those without a means of transportation to base, even a 20-minute drive is a hurdle to utilization of facilities.

Children

The majority of spouses (68 percent) reported that they have at least one minor child living with them at least one-half of the time. Of the total sample, roughly 9 percent reported having a minor child who receives special education or early intervention services or who is in the Exceptional Family Member Program (EFMP).[12] Data from the 2000 Census suggests that military spouses are significantly more likely than spouses of civilians to have preschool children at home, although among the services, Air Force wives are least likely of the military wives to fall into this category (Lim, Golinelli, and Cho, 2007).

Spouse Education and Employment

Virtually all Air Force spouses have at least a high school diploma. Combining educational categories shown in Table 2.2, more than one-third (35.3 percent) of spouses hold a bachelor's or graduate degree, and nearly one-half (45.3 percent) have an associate's degree or have taken some college classes. About one-fifth (20 percent) are currently in school either full or part time. Previous analyses of 2000 U.S. Census data on the spouses of military personnel found similarly high levels of education among Air Force spouses (Lim, Golinelli, and Cho, 2007). That study also revealed that the spouses of military personnel are more highly educated than the spouses of their civilian counterparts and that Air Force wives are the most highly educated of all wives (Lim, Golinelli, and Cho, 2007).

More than one-half of all spouses of active-duty airmen report at least part-time employment, with 42 percent working full time and 14 percent working part time. By definition, dual-military spouses are working at least part time. Again providing context based on 2000

---

[9]   Because the samples were small, the study's analyses of husbands of military members were unable to obtain reliable results by service.

[10]   This study did not report metropolitan residence rates for husbands.

[11]   The percentage of CONUS airmen in the weighted sample does not reflect the population percentage of CONUS airmen because residential status was not used in the creation of the sample weights. Thus, the sample is not balanced on this characteristic.

[12]   Roughly 1 percent of the sample identified themselves as falling into this special needs-EFMP category, and fewer than 1 percent reported that another adult in the household does.

Census data, military spouses are less likely than spouses of civilians to be employed, although Air Force wives are slightly more likely to be employed than other military wives (Lim, Golinelli, and Cho, 2007). Compared to spouses of civilians, military spouses also have a higher unemployment rate, that is, not employed but seeking work; however, the rates for Air Force wives stand closer to those of civilians' wives (Lim, Golinelli, and Cho, 2007).

Although Air Force wives are more likely to be employed and have lower unemployment rates, their average wages are the lowest among the military spouses (Lim, Golinelli, and Cho, 2007). When both hourly wage and yearly income are considered, spouses of military personnel earn less than spouses of civilians, and men earn more than women (Lim, Golinelli, and Cho, 2007).

Among employed spouses in this Air Force survey, the most frequently cited primary reason for working was for personal satisfaction (26 percent). However, more than 40 percent selected one of the two items that reflect financial necessity: either to provide one-half or more of the family income or to supplement the family income to cover basic living expenses (Figure 2.2). Among only spouses who reported working full-time, the most commonly cited primary reason for working is to provide one-half or more of the family's income (28 percent). Among only spouses who report working part-time, supplementing a spouse's income to cover basic living expenses (30 percent) was the most commonly cited primary reason for working.

In Figure 2.2 and other figures in this report, the black bars in the center of each response category indicate the 95-percent confidence interval around each percentage. This is the range of values generally consistent with the results we obtained here and are used to show the degree of uncertainty in these estimates that exists because a limited number of spouses, rather than

Figure 2.2
Employed Air Force Spouses' Primary Reason for Working

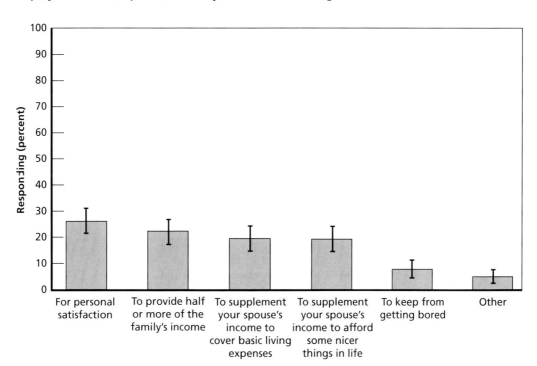

RAND *TR879-2.2*

all, were surveyed. Throughout this report, we present weighted results with these confidence intervals.[13]

Deployment in the Previous Two Years

Air Force leaders are concerned about how recent deployments have affected Air Force families. In April 2010, 39,100 airmen were deployed, with more than 50 percent serving tours longer than four months and about 5 percent serving year-long tours (Tan, 2010). The number of airmen deployed had surged (19 percent since December 2009) to meet the larger Department of Defense (DoD) demand for increased troop levels in Afghanistan (Tan, 2010). Those considered in need of greatest relief were those serving six months, home for six months, and then returning for another six-month deployment (Tan, 2010). Some additional statistics on deployment are derived from survey data the Defense Manpower Data Center (DMDC), collected in August 2009. In the 24-month period prior to the survey, 37 percent of active-duty airmen had been deployed longer than 30 consecutive days, and 57 percent had been deployed at least once since September 11, 2001 (DMDC, 2010, pp. 114, 158).

To help assess how deployments influenced family problems, we asked each spouse whether there had been a 30-day or longer deployment in the family in the previous two years. In 61 percent of dual-military families, at least one spouse had gone on such a deployment. For 22 percent of these couples, both spouses had recently deployed; for 16 percent, only the respondent had recently deployed; and for 23 percent, only the nonrespondent spouse had deployed. Forty-seven percent of civilian spouses reported that their airman spouse had deployed in the past two years.

Demographics

The primary subgroups of interest to the research sponsor were spouses of officers and spouses of enlisted airmen, dual-military spouses and civilian spouses, respondents who live on base and those who do not, and respondents who live with minor children and those who do not. We examined how the descriptive statistics above varied among these four key dimensions.[14] Below, we report only statistically significant differences across subgroups.[15]

Spouses of Officers and Spouses of Enlisted Airmen

Spouses of officers tended to be older, more educated, less likely to be currently enrolled in school, less likely to live on base, and less likely to be in dual-military marriages than their enlisted counterparts. On average, spouses of officers in our sample were 36 years old; spouses of enlisted averaged 31.2. More officers' spouses held bachelor's and graduate or professional degrees than spouses of enlisted airmen (37.7 and 19.1 percent, respectively, for bachelor's; 34.0 and 4.8 percent, respectively, for graduate or professional), but about twice as many spouses

---

[13] Technically, a 95-percent confidence interval indicates the true values for the full population of married active-duty Air Force personnel that are consistent with the observed data from the sample.

[14] Because the OCONUS sample was small, we do not present results for this subgroup. Results for families that have experienced a recent deployment are addressed within the sections on child, spousal employment, and financial problems.

[15] We define a difference as statistically significant when there is no overlap in the 95-percent confidence intervals around each estimate.

of enlisted airmen reported attending school part-time (13.7 for enlisted and 5.7 percent for officers' spouses). Significantly fewer spouses of officers than enlisted live on base (12.9 and 28.9 percent, respectively), and officers' spouses were less likely to be in dual-military marriages (14.3 and 22.2, respectively). No differences were found between the percentage of spouses of officers who have minor children at home and the percentage of spouses of enlisted airmen who do.

Dual-Military and Civilian Spouses

Dual-military spouses differed significantly from civilian spouses on many demographic dimensions: gender, education, residence, parenthood, employment, and whether they were married to officers or enlisted airmen. In our sample, significantly more dual-military than civilian spouses were male (43.9 and 9.3 percent, respectively). That such a large majority of civilian spouses are female reflects the disproportionate representation of men in the Air Force: 85.3 percent of married active-duty officers and 82.7 percent of married active-duty enlisted are male (AFPC, 2010).[16] Fewer dual-military spouses held bachelor's degrees than civilians (16.2 and 25.4 percent, respectively), and slightly fewer held less than a high school diploma (0.9 for dual-military and 0 percent for civilian spouses). Fewer dual-military spouses than civilian spouses reported living on base (13.0 and 28.1 percent, respectively), having a child between the ages of 6 and 18 (30 and 42.6 percent, respectively), and having a child over the age of 18 (1.1 and 5.7 percent, respectively). Dual-military spouses were much more likely to be in school part time than civilian spouses (28.4 and 7.5 percent, respectively). Level of employment also varied: Dual-military spouses were more likely than civilian spouses to be employed full-time (73.9 and 33.9 percent, respectively) and less likely to be employed part-time (3.8 and 16.5 percent, respectively).[17] Dual-military spouses were less likely to be married to officers than were civilian spouses (16.6 and 25.5 percent, respectively). No other significant demographic differences emerged between dual-military and civilian spouses.

Although the survey did not ask the service or component of the second spouse in dual-military couples, Air Force personnel data reveal the demographics of the spouses of the 39,397 dual-military active-duty airmen. Table 2.3 shows the military status of dual-military spouses by component and Air Force or non–Air Force affiliation. Summing some of these data, 96 percent of both dual-military officers and dual-military enlisted are married to another member of

---

[16] Including married and not married airmen, 81.4 percent of active-duty officers and 80.5 of active-duty enlisted are male (AFPC, 2010).

[17] We would expect all dual-military spouses to be employed at least part-time (reservists) if not full-time (reservists and active duty), yet only 77.7 percent of dual-military spouses reported being employed. For weighting and analysis purposes, individuals were characterized according to their military status in the official personnel file as of April 2009. Clearly, some spouses may have joined or left the military between April and the July-August survey administration window, but since the survey asks about problems in the previous year, we believe that using the April status is the better option. Yet when we calculated the employment status using the spouse's military status reported in the survey, still only 81.7 percent of dual-military spouses reported themselves as employed. We suspect that some respondents interpreted the question to mean "employed outside of the military," but we have no way of knowing whether this was the case. There was a similar irregularity, although to a lesser degree, in responses to a spousal employment item on DMDC (2010), which provided distinct "employed" and "armed forces" response options. Although 89 percent of dual-military service members indicated that their spouse was in the armed forces and 5 percent indicated that their spouse was employed, 2 percent reported that their spouse was unemployed and that 4 percent reported their spouse was not in the labor force (i.e., not employed and not seeking, wanting, or needing to work) (DMDC, 2010, p. 26).

Table 2.3
Military Status of U.S. Airmen's Spouses in Dual-Military Households, by Rank of Airman and Component and Air Force Affiliation of Spouse

Component or Air Force Affiliation of Dual-Military Spouse	Active-Duty Air Force	
	Officers (percent)	Enlisted (percent)
Active-duty Air Force	74	87
Air Force reserves or Air National Guard	22	9
Active-duty, other service	4	3
Guard or reserve, other service	0[a]	0[a]
Total	100	100

SOURCE: AFPC, 2010.

[a] Although there are some, they comprise less than one percent.

the Air Force, and 78 percent of officers and 90 percent of enlisted are married to someone on active duty in any service (although nearly all to airmen).

Residence On or Off Base

Spouses living on base were younger, slightly less educated, less likely to be in a dual-military couple, less likely to be married to an officer, and far less likely to be working full-time than their counterparts living off base. Spouses who live on base tended to be a bit younger than those living off base (30.3 and 33.0 years on average, respectively). While 10.5 percent of spouses living on base were part of a dual-military couple, 23.5 percent of those off base were. It is also significant that 12.2 percent of all on-base spouses were married to officers but that 27.6 percent of all off-base spouses were. Slightly more living on base rather than off lacked a high school diploma (1.0 and 0 percent, respectively), and fewer held a graduate or professional degree than those who did (5.3 and 14.0 percent, respectively). Significantly fewer on-base spouses reported working full time than those who lived off base (25.8 and 47.4 percent, respectively). No other significant demographic differences emerged between on- and off-base spouses.

Those With Children and Those Without

Only one significant demographic difference emerged between spouses with and without minor children at home, and it was one of great magnitude. More parents than nonparents lacked a high school diploma (1.1 and 0 percent, respectively).

Subgroup Differences in Survey Responses

Because the population of active-duty airmen and their spouses is diverse, we examined for each survey item whether the results varied across the key demographic characteristics discussed above. Throughout this document, we present only the statistically significant differences among subgroups.

CHAPTER THREE

Problems Related to Children, Finances, Spouse's Employment, and Associated Factors

One of the main goals of the survey was to improve understanding of the problems Air Force families face. The survey focused on problems respondents may have had in the past year in three domains: children, finances, and employment. Figure 3.1 depicts the percentage of spouses in the weighted sample who reported at least one problem in each of the three domains, as well as the percentages for parents and nonparents. Considering the weighted spouse population as a whole, 37 percent of spouses reported at least one problem related to children; 37 percent reported at least one problem related to employment; and 26 percent reported at least one problem related to finances.

Among parents in our weighted sample,[1] problems related to the children were the most prevalent. As shown in Figure 3.1, 55 percent of parents only, reported at least one family prob-

Figure 3.1
Percentage of Spouses Reporting Any Problem in Any Domain, by Parental Status

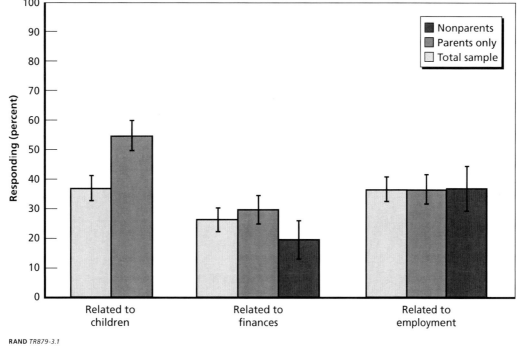

RAND TR879-3.1

---

[1] *Parents* are defined as persons having custody of minor children.

lem related to children. Parents and nonparents did not significantly differ in the likelihood of reporting at least one problem related to employment (37 percent) or at least one financial problem (30 and 20 percent respectively, which was, again, not a statistically significant difference). We next address each problem domain independently to reveal what specific problems families are facing, how deployment may have affected those problems, and what factors respondents believe are associated with the problems they have encountered.

Children

Child Care, Education, and Well-Being for Military Children

The military's child-care system is the largest in the country, and its quality compares favorably with that of civilian child care. DoD continues to promote high-quality care through its inspection and certification system for child-care providers and facilities, financial incentives for providers to achieve accreditation from the National Association for the Education of Young Children, and caregiver training and compensation that improve staff quality and reduce turnover (Pomper et al., 2005, p. 3). Meanwhile, progress in developing affordable, accessible, and high-quality child care in the civilian sector "has been seriously stalled by stagnant funding at the federal level and strained state budgets, with many states now moving backwards in their efforts" (Pomper et al., 2005, p. 15).

Evaluations of the capacity of child care, however, find both sectors lacking: "There is not nearly enough high-quality child care in the United States, even for families who can afford to pay the higher cost, including those military families eligible for the DoD fee assistance program" (Smith and Sarkar, 2008, p. 6). Military child-care centers are heavily subsidized; this, combined with quality and a location convenient to many families translates into great demand and long waiting lists, particularly for infants (Zellman et al., 2009).

Lack of child care can become an issue for military readiness. In one 2004 survey of military parents, single parents and dual-military spouses reported that lack of child care had kept them from reporting for duty, particularly due to lengthy searches for appropriate care following a birth or a permanent change of station (PCS) (Zellman et al., 2009). Furthermore, military parents—mothers in particular—may also find themselves late for work or missing work due to child-care issues (Zellman et al., 2009). Finally, nearly 9 percent of parents had an unmet child-care need, and 22 percent would prefer a different child-care arrangement than the one they had (Zellman et al., 2009).

In addition to frequent moves that require new schools, new friendships, and new neighborhoods, military life often requires parents and children to be apart for extended periods. A separation may be relatively short—a period of long work hours or temporary schooling, training, or other duties away from home—or quite long—while the service member is on an unaccompanied overseas tour or a deployment. As a consequence, military parents may have to miss important holidays, events, and milestones in their children's lives.

Research on how parental deployments to Iraq and Afghanistan have affected the well-being of military children is just emerging and has had mixed results. The children of military personnel deployed to war zones face the possibility that their parents may never come home or may come home injured. Evidence further suggests that many of these children may have parents suffering from traumatic brain injury and/or the psychological effects of war (Tanielian and Jaycox, 2008; Hoge et al., 2004).

Children may have difficulties adapting to parental absence and the family stress associated with deployments to Iraq and Afghanistan (Chandra et al., 2010; Chandra, Hawkins and Richardson, 2010; Ender et al., 2007; Flake et al., 2009, Lipari et al., 2010). Analyses of DMDC's 2008 Active Duty Spouse Survey data suggested that a second deployment might increase the number of child problems exhibited (Lipari et al., 2010). That study also found that families that had experienced three deployments reported fewer child problems, suggesting either that children eventually adapt to deployments or that families whose children do not do so leave the service or change jobs to avoid a third deployment (Lipari et al., 2010).

Air Force Child-Related Services

Our survey asked only about child-related issues that fall under the purview of Airman and Family Services. The Air Force provides traditional child care through child development centers on base, child care in family homes, and school age programs in on-base youth centers, all of which must be accredited. Nontraditional child-care options include, for example, limited, no-cost, extended child care in family homes to accommodate extended work schedules, emergencies, and evening or weekend care. The Returning Home Care Program provides airmen with 16 hours of free child care following deployments of 30 days or more to allow spouses a chance to reconnect with one another following their separation. Other child-care programs offer subsidies for child care in family homes, short-term care for stressed or busy parents, and 20 hours of free care per child during the 60 days before and after a PCS move from one base to another.

Youth programs are aimed at school-aged children. These include child care and activities in five core areas:

1. character and leadership development
2. the arts
3. youth sports, fitness, and recreation
4. health and life skills
5. education and career development.

Air Force school liaison officers help parents manage such issues as school enrollment; incongruent graduation requirements following a move; and helping schoolteachers, counselors, and administrators understand some of the typical behaviors children who have a deployed parent may display.

The survey covered different types of child-related problems a family may be facing that Air Force services have been designed to address:

1. child care
2. activities for children
3. educational issues
4. emotional and behavioral well-being.

The results point to the areas that may benefit from additional assistance or increased awareness of available assistance.

Specific Child-Related Problems and Subgroup Variations

Table 3.1 presents the individual survey items ordered from the largest to the smallest percentages of respondents who report having these child-related problems in the past year. These questions were asked only of the 68 percent of spouses who reported living with a minor child at least half-time. The problems reported most frequently were those associated with finding child care, children's emotional and behavioral well-being, and finding activities for children.

The problem cited most frequently was difficulty finding child care, specifically so that the respondent could accomplish other tasks or take care of him or herself or other people (not including children). Roughly 22 percent of parents in the sample indicated that this was a problem. Additionally, 18 percent of parents indicated that finding child care while working or attending school was also a problem.

Twenty percent of all parents had problems related to a child's emotional or behavioral well-being. However, such problems were more common among parents of a child receiving special education or early intervention services or a child who is a member of the EFMP. Among these parents, 34 percent reported that a child had had emotional or behavior problems in the past year.

The third most frequently cited problem was finding activities for children, with 19 percent of parents noting the difficulty of finding activities that keep children safe or busy during after-school hours or on weekends and 17 percent reporting the same about opportunities for skill development outside school.

Table 3.1
Percent of Spouses Reporting Child-Related Problems

Child-Related Problem	Proportion of Weighted Sample with Minor Child(ren) at Home (percent)	95 percent Confidence Interval (percent)[a]
Obtaining child care so you can get other things accomplished or take care of yourself or people other than your children	21.6	17–26
Child's emotional or behavioral problems	20.4	16–24
Finding activities to keep children safe or busy after school or on weekends	18.7	15–23
Obtaining child care while you work or attend school	18.4	15–22
Finding activities to develop skills outside of school	16.5	13–20
Child's academic performance in school	13.7	10–17
Getting help communicating with schools about school-related issues	9.3	6–12
Getting assistance managing home schooling or enrolling in public or private school	5.0	3–7
Managing a child's special needs[b]	2.6	0–3

NOTE: Survey items asked only of respondents with children under age 18 living with them at least half time.

[a] The true values for the full population of married active-duty Air Force personnel that are consistent with the observed data from the sample.

[b] Only asked of those with a special needs child. Of parents with such a child, 31 percent reported this as a problem.

The fewest parents overall (2.6 percent) reported difficulty managing a child's special needs. However, this issue is especially relevant for those with special needs children or children in EFMP. Within this subset, 31 percent reported that managing a child's special needs was a problem, making it the problem members of this group reported most frequently.

The subgroup analysis found only two statistically significant differences in the types of problems that parents reported. First, spouses of enlisted airmen were more likely than spouses of officers to report difficulty finding activities to keep children safe or busy after school (21.7 and 9.2 percent, respectively). Second, more dual-military spouses than civilian spouses reported that obtaining child care while they worked or attended school was a problem (28.6 and 15.9 percent, respectively). More of those who lived less than 30 minutes from a base report having difficulty finding child care while they worked or attended school than spouses who lived in excess of 30 minutes from a base (21.3 and 8.6 percent, respectively). There were no significant differences between those who lived less than 30 minutes away from base and those who lived more than 30 minutes away in terms of the percentage who worked or attended school either full or part time.

Child-Related Problems and Deployment

We asked the following question of parents in our sample in whose family at least one of the two spouses had deployed for 30 or more days at least once in the past two years and at least one child-related problem listed in the survey had occurred[2]: "Overall, were the child-related problems you experienced worse or better during your or your spouse's last deployment?" The majority of respondents believed that their child-related problems worsened (Figure 3.2). However a large percentage, 41 percent, reported that the deployment did not affect the severity of the child-related problems they faced. Only 7 percent thought their child-related problems improved during their or their spouse's last deployment.

Only one subgroup difference on this item appeared. Although no spouses living on base indicated that their child-related problems improved during their or their spouse's recent deployment, 11 percent of spouses living off base did report improvement.

Factors Associated with Child-Related Problems

The survey asked respondents whether they believed certain factors were associated with their child-related problems, and respondents were allowed to select as many as they thought played a role. The factors the survey included were ones Air Force services attempt to address in some manner. Figure 3.3 shows the percentage of respondents who chose each item as relevant for their child-related problems. These survey items were asked only of parents who reported at least one child-related problem (37 percent of the weighted sample). A recent move or PCS was the factor most frequently cited (33 percent), followed closely by spouse work schedules (30 percent). Approximately 25 percent associated Air Force child-care availability and location with their problems. Also, 10 percent said Air Force child care was too far from work, and 15 percent said it was too far from their child's school. Similar percentages reported that their child-related problems were associated with the kind of activities Air Force youth programs offered and/or the inability of Air Force programs to help manage their child's educational issues.

---

[2] Approximately 20 percent of the total weighted survey sample met the criteria for this question.

Figure 3.2
Change in Child-Related Problems During Deployment

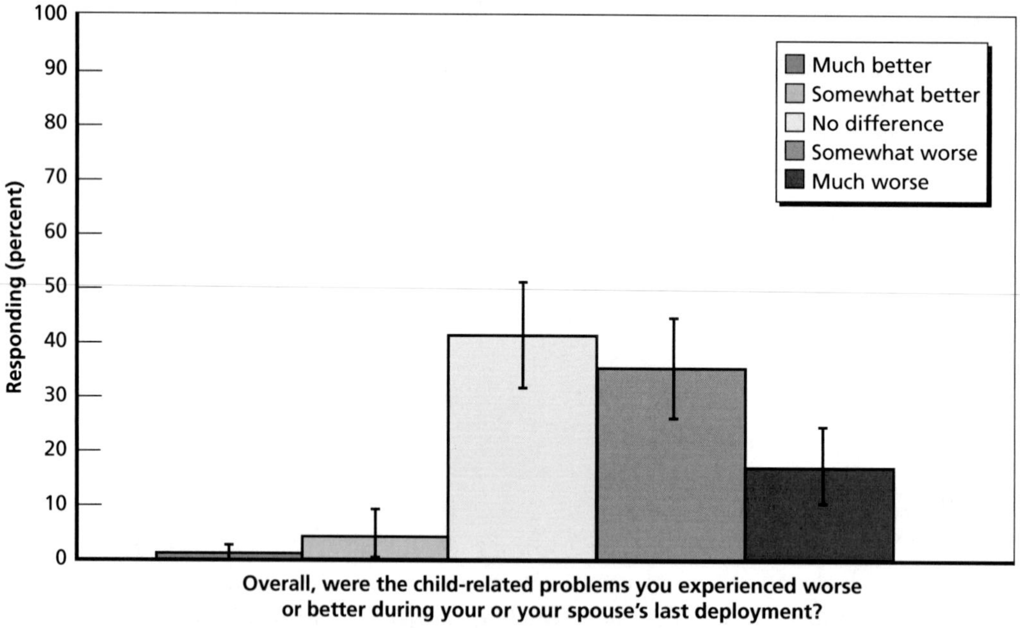

NOTE: Question asked only of respondents who had children and reported child-related problems and who had been deployed at least 30 days in the past two years or who had an active-duty spouse who had been deployed at least 30 days in the past two years (20 percent).
RAND *TR879-3.2*

Three subgroup differences emerged among the reasons that spouses cited for their child-related problems. First, roughly one-half of all spouses of officers attributed their problems to a recent move or PCS, while just over one-quarter of spouses of enlisted airmen did so (48.5 and 28.9 percent, respectively). One explanation for this would be that officers move more frequently, and Air Force administrative data and the August 2009 DMDC survey data indeed support this (AFPC, 2010; DMDC 2010, p. 107).[3] Second, more dual-military than civilian spouses reported two related factors as contributing to their child-related problems: work schedules (48.5 and 24.7 percent, respectively) and the hours that Air Force child care was available (50.8 and 15.8 percent, respectively). That one-half of dual-military spouses related Air Force child-care hours to their child-related problems means that the care currently available is not meeting the needs of a sizable portion of this subpopulation.

---

[3] In Air Force personnel data, 35 percent of officers have been at current stations less than a year; 28 percent, one year; 18 percent, two years; 11 percent, three years; and 8 percent, four years or longer (AFPC, 2010). Among enlisted, 32 percent have been at current stations less than a year; 23 percent, one year; 16 percent, two years; 12 percent, three years; and 17 percent (more than twice as much as officers), four years or longer (AFPC, 2010). Based on DMDC survey data, 37 percent of junior enlisted airmen (pay grades E1–E4) and 92 percent of NCOs (E5–E9) reported ever PCSing. Eighty-four percent of junior officers (O1–O3) and 99 percent of senior officers (O4–O6) reported ever PCSing.

Figure 3.3
Factors Associated with Child-Related Problems

Were any of the following issues associated with the
child-related problems you have had in the past year?

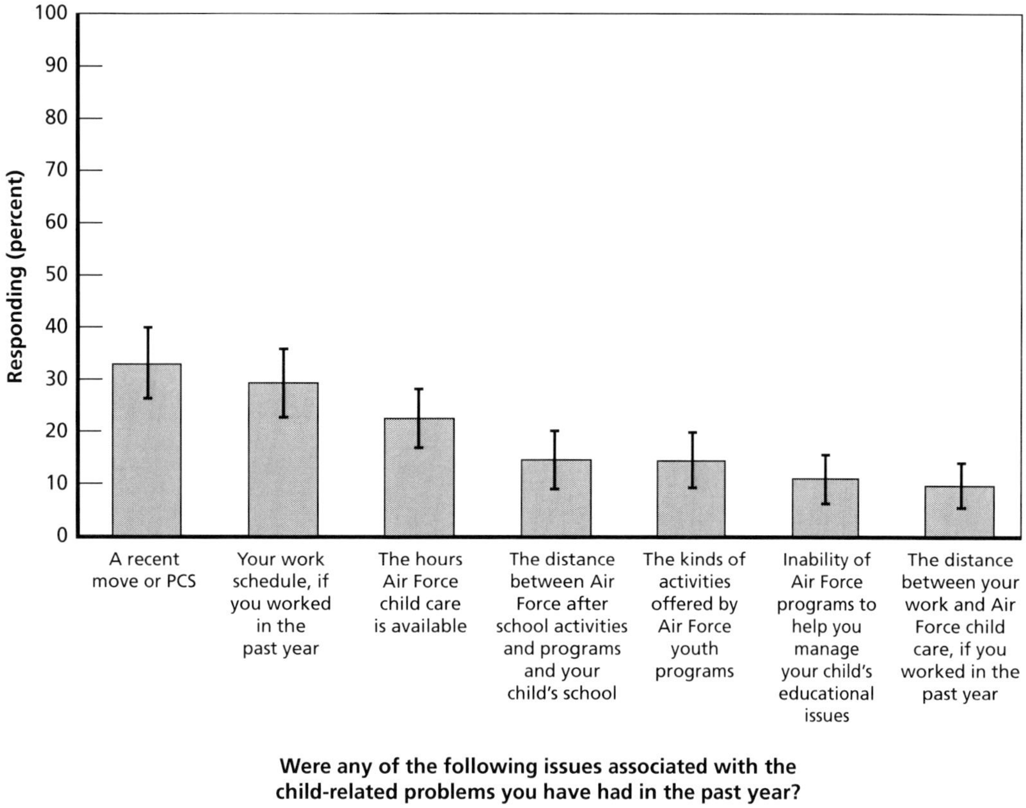

RAND *TR879-3.3*

Finances

Military Financial Problems

Although military service provides some degree of financial stability for military families, these families are not immune to economic trends in the United States. Media reports show that foreclosure rates in towns surrounding military bases are as much as four times as high as the national average and describe military personnel as unable to sell their homes or as selling them at a loss following a geographic reassignment (Finney, 2010; Howley, 2008; Zoroya, 2008). In response, Congress included language in the economic stimulus package to compensate family members who sell their homes at a loss or whose homes are foreclosed on because of a base closure, reassignment, or relocation required for combat wound treatment (Lazo, 2009). Prior to the Protecting Tenants of Foreclosure Act of 2009 (enacted two to three months before our respondents were surveyed), some families faced eviction when the home they were renting was foreclosed on (Carden, 2009). Even before the economic crisis, DoD documented predatory lending practices that targeted young military members and their dependents with high-interest payday loans, car-title loans, "military installment loans," tax refund anticipation loans, and rent-to-own lending (DoD, 2006). Thus, we were particularly interested to learn how Air Force families are faring financially.

Air Force Financial Education Programs and the Air Force Aid Society

Airman and Family Readiness Centers offer airmen and their spouses services to help them manage their financial readiness. Services include one-on-one financial counseling and education on such topics as managing a checkbook, building good credit, consumer awareness, predatory lending, and financial planning and management. These services are offered at no cost to airmen and/or their spouses. Families in financial crises with emergency needs can apply to the Air Force Aid Society for assistance. In 2009, 17,319 airmen received $12.2 million in the form of $11.5 million in interest-free loans and $689,000 in grants.[4]

Specific Financial Problems and Subgroup Variation

The survey listed four possible financial problems: bankruptcy; home foreclosure; trouble paying debt, bills, or a mortgage; and inability to save money.

The good news is that, even following the economic downturn and housing market collapse of 2008, the most common financial problem (nearly 25 percent) was being unable to save money (see Table 3.2), not foreclosure. The next most common problem was trouble paying debt, bills, or a mortgage (roughly 9 percent). The most severe financial problems, home foreclosure and bankruptcy, were rarely reported, with fewer than 1 percent of respondents reporting that either had occurred in the past year.

Subgroup analyses found that the groups more likely to have experienced any financial problem in the last year were spouses of enlisted airmen rather than spouses of officers (30.5 and 12.8 percent, respectively), civilian spouses rather than dual-military spouses (29.5 and 13.3 percent, respectively), and spouses living on base rather than those living off base (35.9 and 23.1 percent, respectively). Among financial problems, spouses of enlisted airmen were more likely than spouses of officers to report a home foreclosure (0.01 and 0.001 percent, respectively); trouble paying debt, bills, or a mortgage (10.7 and 3.3 percent, respectively); bankruptcy (1.1 and 0 percent, respectively); and trouble saving money (28.0 and 12.1 percent, respectively). For those same problems, civilian spouses were more likely than dual-military spouses to report trouble paying debt, bills, or a mortgage (10.2 and 4.0 percent, respectively) and trouble saving money (27.1 and 12.7 percent, respectively). Spouses who lived on base were more likely to report being unable to save money than spouses who lived off base

Table 3.2
Percent of Spouses Reporting Financial-Related Problems

Financial-Related Problem	Proportion of Weighted Sample (percent)	95 percent Confidence Interval (percent)[a]
Inability to save money	24.2	20–28
Trouble paying debt, bills, or a mortgage	8.9	7–11
Foreclosure on a home	0.8	0–2
Bankruptcy	0.7	0–2

[a] The true values for the full population of married active-duty Air Force personnel that are consistent with the observed data from the sample.

---

[4]   A fact sheet is available on the Air Force Aid Society's website.

(35.2 and 20.6, respectively), but no other significant differences emerged. Spouses with custody of minor children were also more likely than those without to report a home foreclosure (1.0 and 0 percent, respectively) and bankruptcy (1.1 and 0 percent), but no significant differences were observed for the other two financial-related problems.

Financial Problems and Deployment

One way the military attempts to compensate service members and their families for the hardships of separation and the danger of deployments is through additional pay entitlements. Deployed troops may be eligible for a family separation allowance, hostile fire or imminent danger pay, hardship duty location pay, and tax free income while serving in a combat zone, to include tax-free reenlistment bonuses. At the same time, the earnings of spouses back home may decline, particularly for spouses who become single parents during a deployment and may need to scale back the number of hours they work to cover the familial role of the deployed spouse.

Spouses who reported at least one financial problem in the past year and whose family had at least one spouse deploy for more than 30 days in the past two years were asked whether their financial problems changed during the last deployment. Figure 3.4 shows that the most common spouse response was that deployment made no difference (36 percent). Twenty-nine percent reported that financial problems worsened during the last deployment, and 35 percent reported that they improved.

Figure 3.4
Ratings of Financial-Related Problems During Deployment

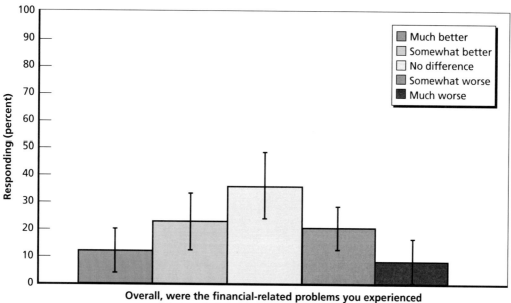

NOTE: Question asked only of respondents had children and reported at least one financial-related problem and whose family had at least one spouse who had been deployed at least 30 days in the past two years (14.5 percent).
RAND *TR879-3.4*

Only one significant subgroup difference was identified: No spouses without children indicated that their financial-related problems were much worse during their or their spouse's recent deployment, but 12 percent of spouses with children did so.

Factors Associated with Financial Problems

Figure 3.5 shows the frequency with which spouses associated various factors with their financial problems (for most, the financial problem was the inability to save money). Respondents were allowed to report as many of these factors as they believed were relevant to their financial problems. The most common responses were the costs related to raising children (64.0 percent), the spouse's employment (47.1 percent), and a recent move or PCS (38.3 percent). Three items addressed Air Force financial educational services: About 30 percent of spouses associated lack of information about these services with their problems and almost 20 percent cited inconvenient access to those programs. About 16 percent of spouses believed that these programs did not address the kinds of problems they faced; this belief, however, might be due to a of lack of information. It may be that spouses simply do not realize that these programs are able to address their concerns and what the programs can do.

Only two significant differences emerged in terms of the reasons spouses cited for their financial problems. First, more civilian spouses than dual-military spouses cited employment

Figure 3.5
Factors Associated with Financial Problems

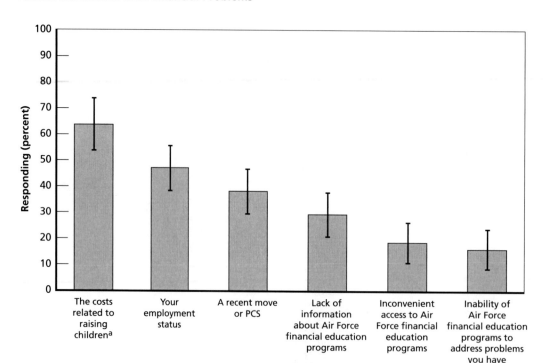

Were any of the following issues associated with the
financial-related problems you have had in the past year?

[a]Question asked only of respondents who had children and reported a financial problem and at least one coresidential child under the age of 18. Among *all* spouses who reported at least one problem, 49.5 percent indicated that the costs of raising children were related to the financial problems.
RAND *TR879-3.5*

status as a cause of their financial problems (50.5 and 17.1 percent, respectively). According to the survey data, significantly fewer civilian than dual-military spouses worked full time (33.9 and 73.9 percent, respectively) or part time (3.8 and 16.5 percent, respectively). Second, more spouses with children indicated that they lacked information about Air Force financial education programs than spouses without children (35.0 and 9.0 percent, respectively).

Employment

Employment of Military Spouses

Relative to spouses of civilians, spouses of military personnel are less likely to be employed, more likely to be jobless but actively looking for work, more likely to be underemployed relative to their professional training, and likely to earn less (Lim, Golinelli, and Cho, 2007; Lim and Schulker, 2010). A recent (2004) interview study found that almost two-thirds of military spouses believed that being married to a service member negatively affected their work opportunities, and few perceived a positive effect (Castaneda and Harrell, 2008). Spouses cited the negative effects of factors long familiar to scholars of military families: frequent and disruptive moves; service-member absences (e.g., for training or deployments); the costs, limited hours, and capacity of child-care facilities; and employer bias against military spouses (Castaneda and Harrell, 2008). Moving every two to three years creates career challenges for spouses, such as the inability to build up workplace seniority, nontransferable college credits or varying degree requirements, or different credentialing or licensing requirements from state to state. One study, however, has argued that military spousal employment research focused on spouse characteristics (e.g., education, seniority) has missed how labor markets around military installations can influence spouses' employment status and earnings (Booth, 2003).[5] Analyses of the 1990 Census demonstrated that the greater the military presence in a geographic area, the lower the average wages of all local women (not just military wives). These analyses also showed that military wives endured greater unemployment and lower income than comparable wives of civilian men (Booth, 2003).

Air Force Spousal Employment Assistance

Spousal employment assistance services, like many other services offered to Air Force spouses, are available for free or at a very low cost. These services include career counseling, résumé development, tips on searching for jobs, guidance on applying for federal employment, workshops on starting small businesses, and information about local employers with job openings.

Specific Employment Problems and Subgroup Variation

Table 3.3 shows spouses' responses to questions about employment problems they may have faced in the past year:

1. finding a job
2. finding the right job
3. having a schedule that allows them to work the hours necessary to meet their financial needs and/or balance time with their families
4. acquiring additional education or training necessary for career development.

---

[5] The vast majority of this work focuses on female spouses rather than on the husbands of women in the military.

Table 3.3
Percent of Spouses Reporting Employment-Related Problems

Employment-Related Problem	Proportion of Weighted Sample (percent)	95 percent Confidence Interval (percent)[a]
Being able to work the number of hours you want or the schedule you want, if you worked in the past year	24.0	20–28
Finding a job that matches your education, abilities, or interests	23.3	20–27
Finding a job in general	19.5	16–23
Being able to get additional education or training for career development	15.9	13–19

[a] The true values for the full population of married active-duty Air Force personnel that are consistent with the observed data from the sample.

The survey asked these questions of all spouses, whether or not they were employed at the time of the survey.

Having at least one problem related to employment in the previous year was significantly more common among civilian than dual-military spouses (40.9 and 20.3 percent, respectively) and among spouses who live on rather than off base (47.4 and 33.2 percent, respectively). Civilian spouses indicated difficulties finding a job more often than dual-military spouses did (24.0 and 2.2 percent, respectively);[6] finding a job that matched their education, abilities, or interests (27.9 and 5.5 percent, respectively); being able to work the hours or schedule they want (27.0 and 13.1 percent, respectively); and being able to get any additional education or training necessary for career development (17.6 and 9.5 percent, respectively). Spouses who live on base were more likely than those off base to indicate problems finding a job that matched their education, abilities or interests (33.0 and 20.0 percent, respectively) and being able to work the hours or schedule they want (37.0 and 19.7 percent, respectively).

Employment Problems and Deployment

When asked about employment-related problems during the last deployment, almost one-half indicated that deployment had no discernable effect on their employment issues (48 percent) (see Figure 3.6). However, more rated their problems as being worse during deployment (44 percent) rather than better (9 percent).

Subgroup analyses revealed that deployments were more likely to exacerbate employment problems for civilian spouses than they were for dual-military spouses. Significantly more civilian than dual-military thought these problems became somewhat worse (28.6 and 6.5 percent, respectively), and fewer civilian than dual-military spouses saw no change (41.8 and 79.3 percent, respectively). So, although nearly 80 percent of dual-military spouses said that deployment did not affect their employment-related problems, almost one-half of civilian spouses reported that deployment did affect their employment negatively.

---

[6]   DMDC's August 2009 Survey of Active Duty Members (2010) asked military personnel questions about their spouse's employment status, which DMDC used to calculate a spouse unemployment rate. The Air Force had the lowest reported percentage of spouses who were not employed but wanting or needing to work: 13 percent, compared to 26 percent of Army spouses, 23 percent of Marine Corps spouses, and 19 percent of Navy spouses.

Figure 3.6
Ratings of Employment Problems During Deployment

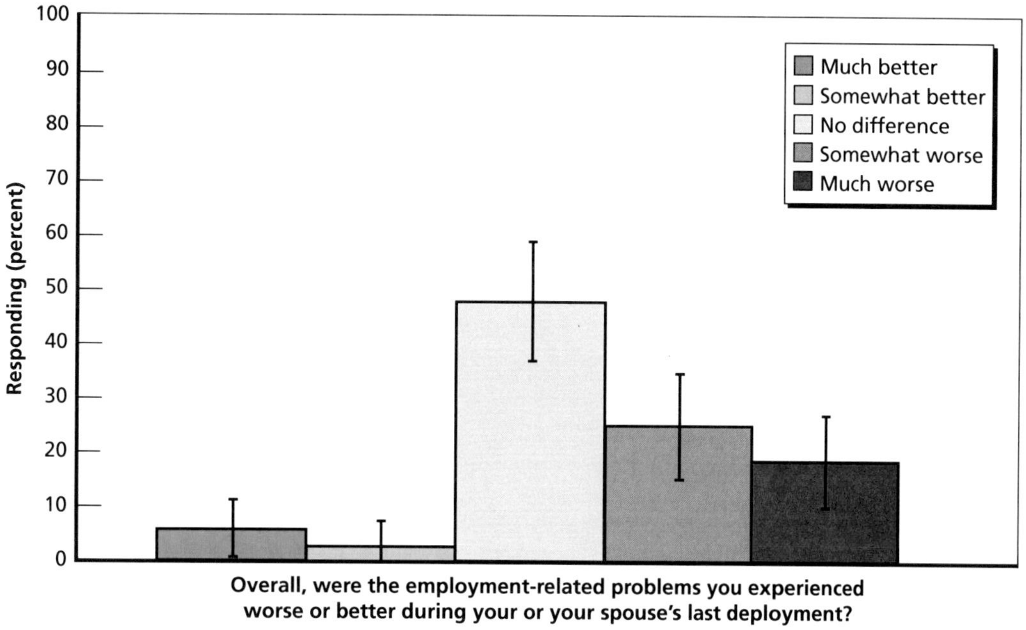

NOTE: Question asked only of respondents who had reported at least one employment-related problem and whose family had at least one spouse who had been deployed at least 30 days in the past two years (16 percent).

RAND *TR879-3.6*

Factors Associated with Employment Problems

Like the factors associated with financial problems, those associated with employment problems focused on child care, residential mobility, and information about Air Force assistance programs (see Figure 3.7). More than 50 percent of spouses related their employment problems to the challenge of finding a job that would cover the cost of child care while they worked. More than 40 percent cited the effects of a recent relocation, and nearly as many reported the difficulty of finding child care available during the hours they needed to work. Around 30 percent reported each of the following about Air Force employment assistance programs: lack of information, inconvenient access, and inability to address their problems. Indeed, the ability of employment assistance services to help the nearly 40 percent of spouses with mismatches between child-care availability and working hours is likely to be limited.

Significant subgroup differences emerged here as well, with spouses who are civilian, living on base, or married to enlisted airmen being much more likely to associate factors on our survey, such as child care or moves, with their employment-related problems. Civilian spouses were more likely than dual-military spouses to cite finding a job that pays enough to cover the cost of child care (59.1 and 25.6 percent, respectively), spouses living on base than off base (73.0 and 45.5 percent, respectively), and spouses of enlisted airmen than spouses of officers (65.2 and 21.6 percent, respectively). In addition, more civilian than dual-military spouses cited the role of a recent move or PCS (47.4 and 23.8 percent, respectively), the inability of Air Force employment assistance programs to address their problems (30.0 and 11.8 percent, respectively), and inconvenient access to Air Force assistance programs (30.5 and 12.1 percent, respectively).

Figure 3.7
Factors Associated with Employment Problems

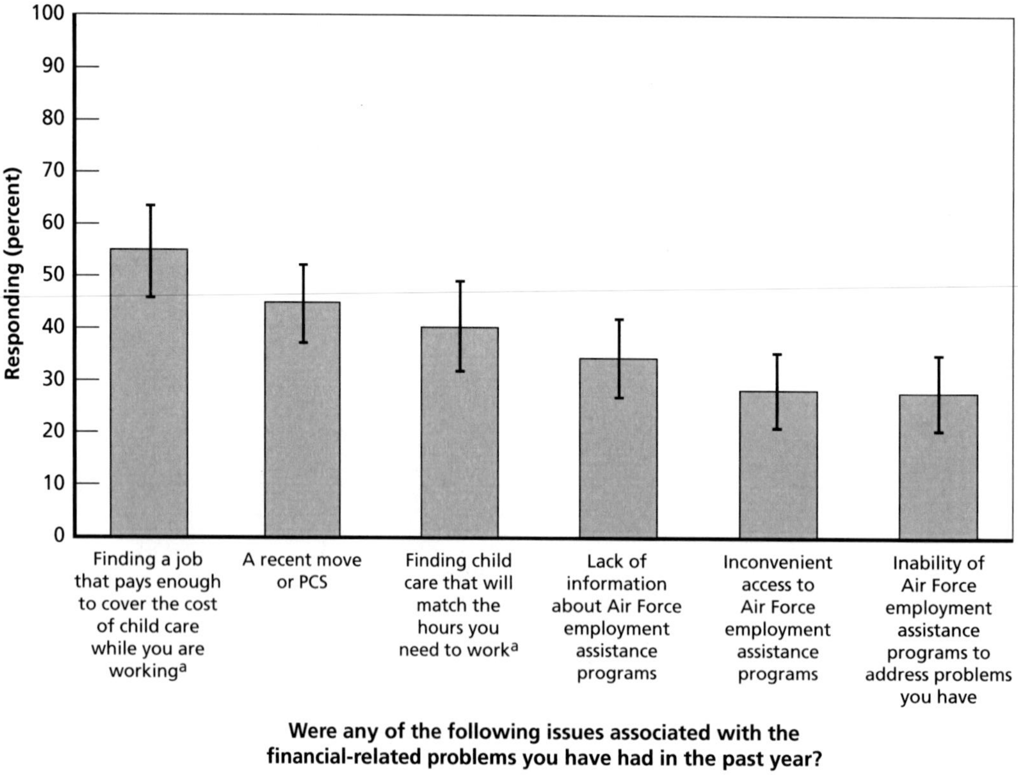

Were any of the following issues associated with the
financial-related problems you have had in the past year?

[a] Question asked only of respondents who had reported at least one employment problem and at least one coresidential child under the age of 18. Among *all* spouses who reported at least one problem, 36.7 percent indicated that finding a job to cover the cost of child care was related to their financial problems, and 27.2 percent indicated that finding child care to match work hours was related to their financial problems.

RAND *TR879-3.7*

Air Force Services to Assist Families with the Potential Negative Effects of Deployments

Many spouses found their problems were worse during the most recent deployment in their family (Figures 3.2, 3.4, and 3.6). This was particularly true for child-related problems. Among parents who experienced a recent deployment, 53 percent reported that problems with children were worse during the latest deployment, and 12 percent reported that financial problems were worse. No nonparent spouses reported worsening of financial problems during their family's last deployment. Among both parents and nonparents combined, 44 percent indicated that employment problems had worsened during a recent deployment.

The Air Force offers support to the families of the deployed. The Armed Forces Crossroads website (2010), the official community website, offers guidelines for pre-, during- and post-deployment challenges and links to many related websites. Many bases offer videoteleconference sites to facilitate family communication during the deployment. Events and special promotions are offered by organizations, such as the Air Force Aid Society, the child-care centers, and the Key Spouse organizations which are made up of volunteer spouses.[7]

Mandatory for airmen, but voluntary for family members, are pre- and postdeployment briefings. Predeployment briefings typically focus on steps family members should take to prepare for separation and the Air Force resources available to support them both formally and informally through the deployment cycle. Briefings for families during a deployment can provide unclassified information about the deployment circumstances, make announcements about community events and merchant specials aimed at families of the deployed, and connect family members having problems to the appropriate support services. Postdeployment briefings typically address issues common for airmen reintegrating into family and civilian life and also advise about formal Air Force resources available to assist with the transition.

This survey asked respondents who had a spouse who had gone on a deployment of 30 or more days in the past two years (approximately 47 percent of the weighted sample) whether or not they had attended any deployment briefings at any time before, during, or after their spouse's last deployment. We chose to set a 30-day deployment minimum for this question because of our presurvey analyses of Air Force deployment data, which suggested that only 35 percent of our sample of married active-duty airmen would fit this category.[8] We were concerned that setting a higher minimum deployment might leave too few eligible respondents. However, given the survey responses (47 percent met the 30-day minimum), we may have been able to solicit sufficient responses with a higher-minimum deployment.

Of the overall eligible sample, 23 percent attended a deployment briefing; however, 34.9 percent of the dual-military and 20.4 percent of the civilian spouses (Figure 3.8) attended. Although this difference appears large, the confidence intervals are just long enough to render it nonsignificant at the 95-percent level. No other significant subgroup differences were detected.

This survey did not provide any information that would allow us to judge how favorable or unfavorable these results might be. It is possible that spouses experienced with deployments are already well-informed about the topics contained in the briefings, or that spouses acquire this information through other channels, such as on Air Force websites or from Air Force friends or neighbors. However, it is also possible that lack of attendance reflects barriers to attendance, such as inconvenient timing, lack of awareness about the occurrence or potential value of the briefings, or the inability to coordinate child care to be able to attend. In some cases, briefings are not available, particularly when airmen deploy individually rather than as part of a unit. It is also possible that spouses are less likely to need deployment support for shorter deployments and that our results would have shown a higher percentage of the population attending deployment-related briefings if we had set a 90-day deployment minimum for respondents, rather than a 30-day minimum.

The survey then asked all respondents whose spouse deployed in the past two years to rate the overall services (not just briefings) provided to their families during the last deployment. Many respondents rated deployment services positively—45 percent rated them as "excellent" or as "good" (Figure 3.9). However, almost 20 percent rated them only "fair" or "poor." Nota-

---

[7]   The Key Spouse program aims, in part, to establish a sense of community among leaders, airmen, and families (Lyle, 2009).

[8]   We deemed the Air Force administrative deployment data unreliable for sampling or weighting because of numerous errors (e.g., deployments dated in the future, deployments starting and ending on the same day). However, we considered the information sufficient to inform construction of this survey item.

Figure 3.8
Percentage Attending Deployment Briefings During Spouse's Last Deployment Cycle, by Dual-Military and Civilian Spouses

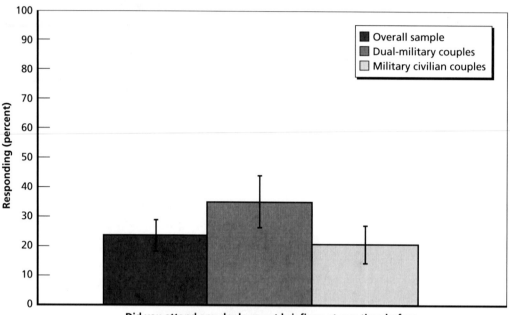

Did you attend any deployment briefings at any time before,
during, or right after your spouse's last deployment?

NOTE: Asked only of respondents whose spouse had been deployed at least 30 days in the past two years.
RAND *TR879-3.8*

Figure 3.9
Spouses' Ratings of Deployment Services

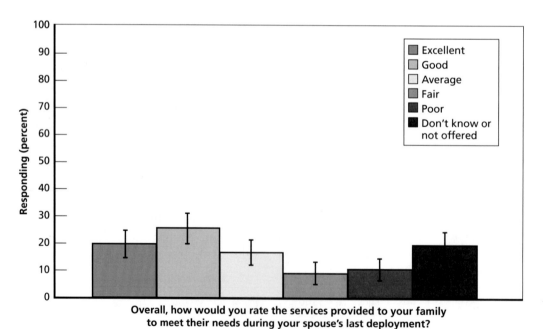

Overall, how would you rate the services provided to your family
to meet their needs during your spouse's last deployment?

NOTE: Asked only of respondents whose spouse had been deployed at least 30 days in the past two years
(47 percent).
RAND *TR879-3.9*

bly, almost 20 percent of spouses who had experienced a deployment were unable to rate deployment services (e.g., did not know the effect, or services were not offered). Spouses of enlisted airmen were more likely than spouses of officers to rate deployment services as "good" (28.5 and 11.8 percent, respectively); however, this statistically significant difference between groups disappears when we collapse the positive ratings (45.2 percent of enlisted spouses and 42.0 percent of officer spouses rate these services as "excellent" or "good").

The survey asked a final deployment-related question of all respondents to test the extent to which they perceived that families received more support for first deployments than for later ones. Opinions were split almost evenly between agreement and disagreement (Figure 3.10), and this variation did not differ significantly by any of our key subgroups. We cannot tell whether those who agreed think this additional support is warranted or not, but it is possible that some find this a source of inequity.

Summary

This survey focused on specific types of problems that Air Force families may face, paying particular attention to how specific elements of Air Force life may contribute to those problems (e.g., deployments) and how specific formal Air Force services may help alleviate them.

The most common problems married Air Force spouses with primary custody of minor children cited were related to the children; more than one-half of parents selected at least one of the problems listed in this category on the survey. Among these, child-care issues, emotional and behavioral problems, and difficulties findings activities for children were the most common. The factors most commonly associated with these child-related problems were a recent move, the spouse's employment schedule, and the hours Air Force child care is avail-

Figure 3.10
Spouses' Perceptions of First Deployment Support

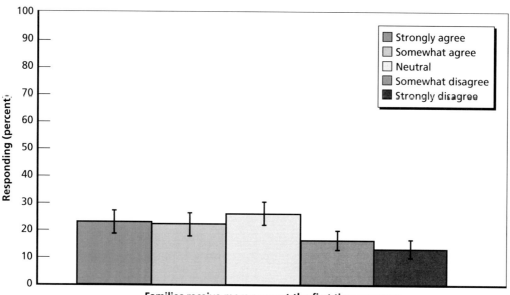

Families receive more support the first time a spouse
is deployed compared to later deployments

able. Among spouses who indicated any such problems, more than one-half reported that they worsened during deployment, although about 40 percent reported no change. On the positive side, more than 40 percent of parents reported experiencing none of the child-related problems included in this survey.

Less than one-third of spouses reported having any of the financial problems on our survey, and the most commonly reported financial problem was the inability to save (almost one-quarter of spouses). For almost one-tenth, bills or debt was a problem. Parents were no more likely than nonparents to report at least one financial problem, although bankruptcy and foreclosure as single events were more likely among those with custody of minor children. Childless spouses rated their financial problems as better or no different during deployment, but more than one-tenth reported finances worsened during deployment. The factors most commonly associated with financial problems were the costs of raising children, spousal employment status, and a recent relocation.

More than one-third of spouses reported at least one employment problem in our survey. Nearly one-quarter found it difficult to working the number of hours or the schedule they desired or to find a job appropriate to their education, skills, or interests. One-fifth had trouble finding any job at all. The most recent deployment had either not changed or had worsened most spousal employment problems. The top factors associated with these problems related to the cost of child care, a recent relocation, or the hours of available child care.

Although more than 60 percent of spouses overall experienced none of the employment problems included in the survey, they were more common among some, civilian spouses in particular. Among civilian spouses, roughly 25 percent reported problems finding a job, and slightly more agreed with items about problems finding a good job match, finding desirable hours or scheduling, or employment problems worsening during their spouse's last deployment. Approximately 60 percent indicated difficulties finding a job that paid enough to cover the cost of child care while they worked, and nearly 50 percent associated a recent move or PCS with their employment problems. Dual-military spouses reported these employment-related problems much less often. Furthermore, about 50 percent of civilian spouses reported that deployment exacerbated these problems, while 80 percent of dual-military spouses reported no effect at all.

Although many Air Force spouses appear to be doing well on the dimensions we assessed, the survey responses indicate room for improvement in some formal Air Force support services designed to prevent or ameliorate some of the most pressing problems that Air Force families may face. About one-third of spouses related their employment or financial problems to lack of information about formal Air Force employment assistance or financial education programs. Smaller percentages reported inconvenient access to these programs or a perception that these programs are unable to meet their specific problems.

Deployment briefings, typically aimed at mitigating some of the negative impact of deployments, were attended by only 23 percent of the eligible survey sample. More dual-military spouses attended these briefings compared to civilian spouses. Despite low levels of attendance, overall deployment support services were rated "good" or "excellent" by 45 percent of respondents whose spouse had recently deployed. Across all spouses surveyed there was variation in whether respondents thought there was a discrepancy in the amount of formal support provided to spouses experiencing their airman's first deployments relative to spouses who had experienced a family deployment before.

We might expect those living further away from base resources to have been more likely to report problems, but that is not what we found. More spouses who live 30 minutes from base than spouses who live further away report problems finding child care while they work or attend school. Eleven percent of parents living off base believed their child-related problems had improved during their or their spouse's deployment, but none of the parents living on base did. Spouses who live on base were more likely than those who live off base to report problems saving money. They were also more likely to report having an employment-related problem, and in particular a problem finding a job matching their education, abilities or interests and a problem being able to work the number of hours or schedule they want. On-base spouses were also more likely than off-base spouses to associate their employment problems with difficulties finding a job that covers the cost of child care while they work. Although spouses on base are physically closer to Air Force resources, they may face more problems than their peers because they are younger and less likely to have a graduate or professional degree. Furthermore, spouses who live on base are more likely to be civilians (one-tenth of our on-base spouses is in a dual-military marriage, compared to one-quarter of our off-base spouses), and thus may be less likely to have learned about base resources through leadership unit announcements or mentoring of subordinates, Air Force training or briefings, or routine exposure to advertisements posted in the workplace.

These data offered insights to Air Force efforts during the Year of the Air Force Family, as leaders aimed to further develop the organization's ability to support its airmen and their families.

CHAPTER FOUR

Selected Support Services, Perceptions About the Leadership, and Satisfaction with Air Force Life

Additional survey items were designed to help the Air Force understand the delivery of services to Air Force families and to offer a sense of overall spouse satisfaction with Air Force life. The research sponsor was interested in learning about how families spend their leisure time, any potential problems that may have arisen from the renaming of the Family Support Center to the Airman and Family Readiness Center that might need to be addressed, and the best way to reach spouses with information about Air Force programs. The survey concluded with general items about spouses' perceptions of Air Force leadership and overall satisfaction with their lives.

Leisure Time

Leisure activities may seem to be all about "fun and games," but they can benefit the health and welfare of participants in multiple ways. Recreational activities can provide opportunities for family members to bond as a unit and to connect with other families, who can provide friendship, support, and advice. Physical fitness activities can relieve stress and can combat a host of health problems, such as obesity, depression, and heart disease (Warburton, Nicol, and Bredin, 2006). Hobbies and recreational classes can build skills and create a sense of pride and accomplishment. Group activities can build social skills and help develop leadership and teamwork abilities.

Air Force services facilitate access to a wide array of activities for airmen and their dependents. The research sponsor selected a subset of these for inclusion in a survey section on leisure activities that spouses and their families enjoy:

1. attending events coordinated by the officers', noncommissioned officers' (NCO), or enlisted club
2. using a local library
3. using a local gym or fitness center
4. participating in outdoor recreation
5. working on and learning arts and crafts in groups
6. using an auto hobby shop to work on or learn how to repair cars
7. facilities for purchasing event tickets or making tour or travel reservations
8. golfing
9. bowling
10. participating in community center activities.

Respondents indicated whether they or any family member had participated in each of the ten types of activities in the past year and, if so, whether they had done so on base, off base, or both. Nearly everyone in the survey reported participation in at least one of these activities (only four respondents, or fewer than 1 percent of our sample, reported no participation at all). Figure 4.1 depicts the percentage of spouses who reported family-member participation in each leisure activity, by location.

Clearly, Air Force offerings are a major source of support for the recreational, hobby, and fitness activities of Air Force families. The majority of families participated in six of the ten types of activities on base: auto hobby shops (which may have few equivalents off base); officers', NCO, and enlisted club–sponsored events; community centers; local libraries; bowling; and local gyms or fitness centers. Respondents reported that one activity, golf, was most commonly done both on and off base, rather than primarily on one or the other. Only 5 percent of our respondents indicated that all their reported leisure activities took place only off base: Compared to the survey sample overall, this group contained significantly more female spouses, more civilian spouses, more spouses of officers, more off-base spouses, more spouses with advanced degrees, and fewer spouses with only some college.

Three types of activities—arts-and-crafts projects, purchasing travel tickets and tour and travel reservations, and outdoor recreation—took place primarily off base. Although it makes sense that many outdoor activities, such as hiking, fishing, hunting, camping, and kayaking, would occur off base, it is not clear why 20.7 percent of families are participating in arts-and-crafts activities with others only off base and not as a part of Air Force–sponsored arts-and-crafts groups. From this survey, we cannot tell whether this is a matter of preference, schedul-

Figure 4.1
Family Participation in Different Types of Leisure Activities in the Past Year, by Location

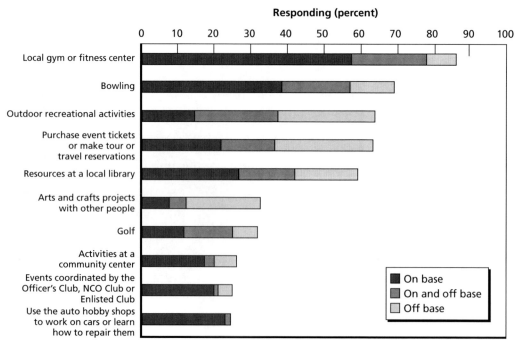

ing incompatibilities, a mismatch between the arts and crafts families enjoy and those offered on base, or a lack of information about on-base classes and activities.

When we considered how many different types of activities each family participated in, we found statistically but not practically significant subgroup differences (Table 4.1). On average, spouses of officers engaged in one more type of activity than did spouses of enlisted airmen. Officers' families were more likely than enlisted families to participate in activities solely off base and to participate in their leisure activities both on and off base. In particular, spouses of officers reported that they or a family member attended events sponsored by the officers' club, NCO club, or enlisted club more often than did enlisted spouses (39.9 and 20.6 percent, respectively), used resources at a local library (73.4 and 54.9 percent, respectively), participated in outdoor recreation activities (73.7 and 61.2 percent, respectively), did arts and crafts with other people (44.2 and 29.6 percent, respectively), purchased event tickets or made travel plans (80.1 and 58.9 percent, respectively), and played golf (42.7 and 29.0 percent, respectively).

Although the overall number of types of activities that dual-military and civilian families participated in did not differ significantly, dual-military spouses were slightly more likely to report participation in activities only on base than civilian spouses and participated in fewer activities only off base. This difference is so small, however, that it does not have much practical relevance. Significantly more dual-military families than civilian families participated in two types of activities: events coordinated by the officers' club, NCO club, or enlisted club (33.7 and 23.0 percent, respectively) and using a local fitness center (95.3 and 84.1 percent, respectively).

Residence on or off base was not differentially associated with the average overall number of types of leisure activities that spouses reported. Families who lived on base, however, engaged in a greater range of activities only on base and participated in significantly fewer types of activities only off base. Conversely, spouses who lived off base participated in more types of activities only off base and fewer only on base.

Parents and nonparents reported involvement in a similar number of types of activities, but those with children participated in significantly more types of activities only off base. Families with children were more likely to participate in arts and crafts with other people than

Table 4.1
Mean Number of Types of Recreation Activities, by Subgroup

For	Total Types of Activities	Number of Activities Conducted		
		Only On Base	Only Off Base	Both On and Off Base
Officers	5.6[a]	2.2	1.9[a]	1.5[a]
Enlisted	4.6	2.4	1.1	1.1
Dual-military	5.2	2.9[a]	1.0[a]	1.3
Civilian spouse	4.7	2.3	1.3	1.1
Lives on base	4.9	3.3[a]	0.6[a]	1.0
Lives off base	4.8	2.1	1.5	1.2
Parents	5.0	2.4	1.4[a]	1.2
Nonparents	4.5	2.3	1.0	1.2

[a] Indicates difference between groups is statistically significant at the 95-percent confidence level.

those without (40.9 and 16.3 percent, respectively) and in activities at a community center (29.5 percent and 18.7 percent, respectively).

The survey asked how satisfied the spouses were with the amount of leisure time their family spent together. Roughly two-thirds of spouses reported being satisfied with the amount of family leisure time they had (Figure 4.2). Approximately equal percentages of respondents in the weighted sample were very satisfied or somewhat satisfied (32 percent). No subgroup differences were observed with respect to satisfaction with family leisure time, not even between parents and nonparents or dual-military and civilian spouses.

The 2006 Name Change from Family Support Center to Airman and Family Readiness Center

The research sponsors in Airman and Family Services wanted to assess the degree to which people were aware that in 2006 the Family Support Centers had been renamed Airman and Family Readiness Centers and whether the name change was confusing or misleading or was an impediment to families being able to find the center for services they might need. The survey found that 61 percent of spouses knew that the name of the Family Support Center had recently changed.[1] Of that group, 19 percent felt that the name change was confusing. Yet

Figure 4.2
Spouses' Satisfaction with Family Leisure Time

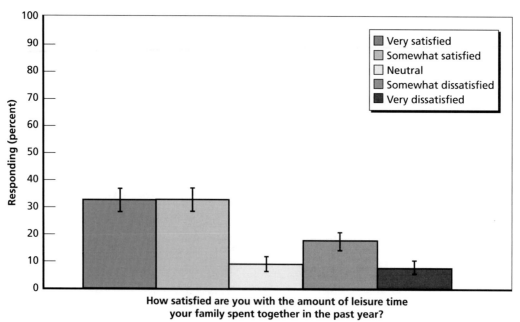

RAND TR879-4.2

---

[1]   The name change took effect in 2006, so it is possible that spouses of airmen who joined the Air Force after 2006 were simply not aware that the Airman and Family Readiness Center had ever been named the Family Support Center. Of those who joined prior to 2007 (i.e., those who should have known about the name change) 60 percent were aware of the name change. Of those who joined in 2007 or later 66 percent knew about the name change. These percentages do not differ if 2006 is used as the cutoff.

fewer than 2 percent reported that the name change had caused problems in finding family support services. Significantly more dual-military spouses than civilian spouses were aware of the change (84.3 and 54.5 percent, respectively). Significantly more spouses who lived on base than who lived off base also knew that the name change had occurred (71.6 and 57.0 percent, respectively).

Preferred Means of Communication About Programs and Services

Staff members in Airman and Family Services offices typically do not just want to wait for family members to seek out information from the Airman and Family Readiness Centers: They want to be able to reach out to family members, keep them up to date, and find out what concerns them. Thus, the staff members would like to know what means spouses would prefer the Air Force use for communicating with them about programs and services. We therefore asked respondents to consider eight means of communication and to indicate up to two that they would prefer to use for learning about these resources. Almost one-half chose email as one of the two (see Figure 4.3). Air Force newsletters and newspapers (37.5 percent) and Air Force websites (30.6 percent) rounded out the top favorites. Despite a strong preference for such electronic tools as email and websites for learning about Air Force programs and services, such social networking tools as Facebook, MySpace, and Twitter were among the least preferred tools.

Figure 4.3
Spouses' Communication Preferences for Learning About Air Force Programs and Services

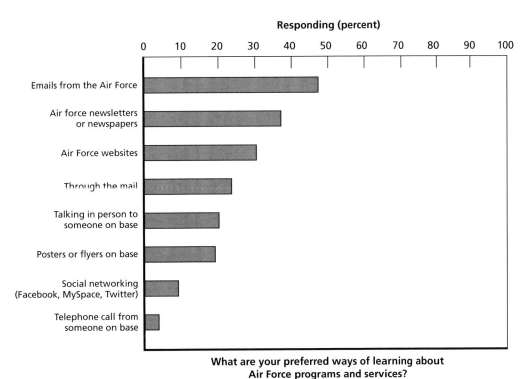

NOTE: Respondents selected up to two items.

RAND *TR879-4.3*

Differences emerged between two particular subgroups on the preferred means of communication. Significantly more civilian spouses than dual-military spouses indicated that their top two preferred ways of learning about Air Force programs and services included direct mailings (28.0 and 8.5 percent, respectively) and Air Force newspapers and newsletters (40.7 and 25.0 percent, respectively). Additionally, significantly more dual-military spouses than civilian spouses selected email (60.0 and 44.5 percent, respectively) and posters or flyers on base (29.3 and 16.9 percent, respectively) as their top two preferred methods of communication. We also found that significantly more spouses of enlisted personnel than spouses of officers preferred direct phone calls (5.0 and 0.7 percent, respectively) and/or talking to someone on base (23.0 and 12.1 percent, respectively) as their primary means of learning about Air Force resources.

Spouses' Perceptions About the Leadership's Concern for Air Force Families

Several survey items assessed whether spouses perceived that Air Force leadership at the supervisor level, the squadron or unit commander level, and the very top of the Air Force cared about their families' well-being. The vast majority of respondents agreed that supervisors and commanders care about their families' well-being (Figure 4.4). Moving furthest away from the level of leadership that spouses might have the opportunity to engage with directly, a majority of respondents (60 percent) agreed that senior leaders at the very top of the Air Force, in Washington, D.C., cared about the well-being of Air Force families, but the level of agreement was lower than with the other leadership questions. Also, more spouses disagreed with this question (22 percent) than with the other support questions. Thus, the higher up the chain of command, the more spouses' perceptions about whether Air Force leaders cared about them varied. We found no significant subgroup differences were found for the leadership support items. On these items, we explored whether there were differences among spouses of junior enlisted airmen (E1–E4), junior NCOs (E5–E6), senior NCOs (E7–E9), company-grade officers (O1–O4), or field-grade officers (O4–O6) (our sample did not include spouses of general officers), but found no significant variation.

Satisfaction

Three survey items asked respondents to rate how satisfied they are with their own lives, with the level of well-being of their families, and with Air Force family life. The majority of spouses of active-duty airmen reported being satisfied with their lives, their family lives, and Air Force family life (Figure 4.5). About 90 percent of respondents agreed strongly or somewhat that they are satisfied with life. More than 90 percent were satisfied with their families' well-being, and 84 percent were satisfied with Air Force family life. We found no significant subgroup differences for the satisfaction survey items. For these items, we also looked for variation by the rank subgroups and found that the only significant difference was that significantly fewer spouses of junior NCOs were "very satisfied" with their lives than were spouses of company grade officers (52.7 and 69.2 percent, respectively).

Figure 4.4
Spouses' Perceptions of Whether Air Force Leadership Cares About Family Well-Being

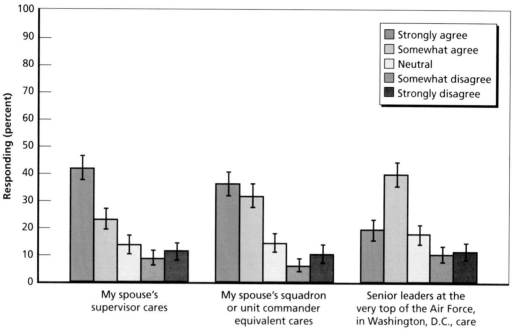

RAND *TR879-4.4*

Figure 4.5
Spouses' Satisfaction with Life, Family Life, and Air Force Family Life

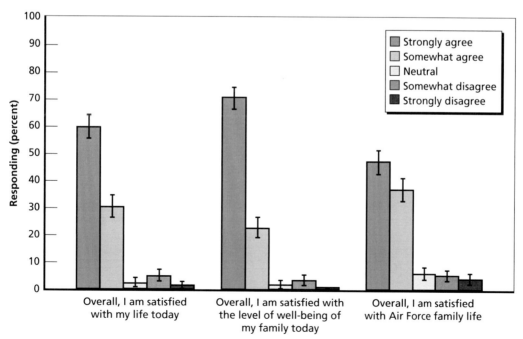

RAND *TR879-4.5*

Organizational Commitment

Finally, the survey asked spouses about the likelihood that their family would remain with the Air Force for another tour of duty. Intentions were high among spouses of active-duty airmen: More than 80 percent estimated the likelihood of their family staying as very likely or somewhat likely (Figure 4.6). The projected likelihood of remaining did not vary significantly by our key subgroups. A closer inspection of this item by rank groups revealed that spouses of senior NCOs, who are likely to be nearing the retirement threshold of 20 years of service, were significantly more likely than officer spouses or junior NCO spouses to say they would be somewhat unlikely or very unlikely to remain in the Air Force. Indeed, 36.2 percent of spouses who believed that they were unlikely to stay were married to senior NCOs, but senior NCO spouses made up only 13 percent of our sample.

Summary

On average, Air Force families participated in five of the ten activities listed on the survey in the past year; in six of these categories, families tended to participate in them primarily on base. Although participation in some of the ten recreational activities included in the survey varied by the subgroups examined, use of a local gym or fitness center and bowling remained the most

Figure 4.6
Spouses' Perceptions of Likelihood Their Family Will Remain in the Air Force

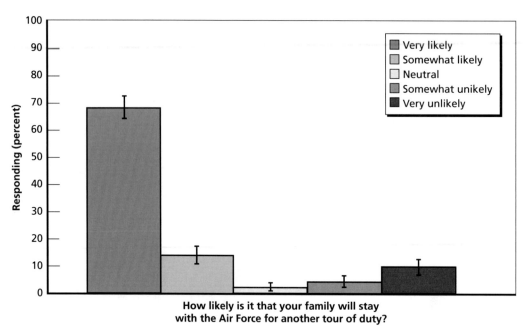

RAND TR879-4.6

popular for all. Further, more than 60 percent of spouses were satisfied with the amount of leisure time their families spent together, and this was consistent across all subgroups.

Airman and Family Readiness Centers provide a number of important resources to Air Force families, which may be especially valuable during deployments. Roughly 60 percent of the sample knew of the name change and, of those, roughly 20 percent felt that the name change was confusing, yet fewer than 2 percent reported this change was a barrier to receiving services.

The survey also asked about preferred means of communication from the Air Force: the channels the Air Force could use to publicize a name change or local events or information on resources available to help them. Two of the three most commonly preferred means of communication were electronic: email (almost 50 percent) and Air Force websites (about 30 percent). Air Force newsletters and newspapers were popular among roughly 40 percent of spouses.

Overall, the majority of spouses felt that Air Force leadership at the supervisor level, the squadron or unit commander level, and at the very top of the Air Force cared about their family's well-being, although this was true to a lesser degree for the highest levels of leadership. Similarly, spouses reported high levels of satisfaction with life, family life, and Air Force family life. Thus, it may not be surprising that roughly 80 percent of spouses reported that another tour of duty was highly or somewhat likely for their family.

So, despite reporting difficulties with child-related, employment, and financial problems and the role moves and deployments played in those problems, Air Force families are highly satisfied with Air Force leadership and Air Force life in general.

CHAPTER FIVE

Recommendations

The survey results presented here were designed to provide Air Force leadership some insights about Air Force families with a weighted sample that would be representative of married active-duty airmen. It also contributes to scholarship on military families, which has rarely focused on Air Force families in particular (exceptions in the last decade include Spera, 2009). The survey instrument focused on specific problems families might be facing and the factors that might be associated with them, family use of recreational services, and attitudes about Air Force leadership and Air Force life. This chapter explores how these findings were offered to help guide organizational efforts during the 2009–2010 Year of the Air Force Family.

Limitations of the Sample

The survey sampling and weighting strategy sought to provide a representative sample of married active-duty airmen, ensuring sufficient numbers of spouses of officers and enlisted airmen, of dual-military and military-civilian couples, those with and without children. As noted previously, weighting of the sample does not ensure representativeness if there are unknown differences related to the questions we addressed between those who participated in the survey and those who were contacted but failed to respond or to complete the survey.

One known limitation of the sample is the underrepresentation of spouses of airmen assigned to OCONUS duty stations. Only 6 percent of the weighted sample of spouses reported living OCONUS, but 22 percent of airmen were assigned OCONUS according to Air Force administration records. Although some spouses do not accompany airmen serving on OCONUS tours, higher rates of incorrect and incomplete contact information in the personnel data files for this population concern us. Survey results may differ for spouses living OCONUS. For example, we might expect the employment challenges to be greater (due to language and work-visa hurdles) or more leisure activities to take place on base (given language barriers in certain locations). Spouses with children who did not accompany their airmen overseas might be more likely to face such problems as child-care issues or emotional problems associated with being separated from a parent. Additionally, previous research focusing on Army spouses living overseas revealed that foreign residence was negatively associated with physical and psychological well-being (although this study also faced challenges contacting spouses overseas and achieving a sufficient response rate) (Burrell et al., 2006). Thus, we believe that a targeted effort exploring whether similar outcomes occur among Air Force spouses would be worthwhile.

Better knowledge of this population would help Air Force services target improvements and plan new developments to support families overseas or separated from their loved ones. For example, in 2009, the Air Force announced expanded opportunities for airmen assigned to unaccompanied year-long tours in Korea to request to extend their tours to two to three years so they can bring their families with them (McKeen, 2009). Expansion of base infrastructure to accommodate these families' needs for housing, schooling, and other activities is planned (McKeen, 2009).

We recommend either an additional survey targeting the spouses of OCONUS airmen or at least a concerted effort to ensure the availability of accurate contact information for any future survey of Air Force spouses. Encouraging frequent updates of contact information and other administrative records for this population would facilitate contact with this particular segment of the Air Force population.

This survey did not assess the experiences and assessments of guard and reserve spouses, although it is likely that some of our dual-military couples include a member of the guard or reserve.[1] Most of the items on this survey could also apply to a reserve population; however, some modifications would be warranted, such as adding "distance to the nearest Air Force base" to the list of possible associated factors and adding a few demographic items to determine how far away from a base the spouse lives, whether the airman was mobilized in the past year, and the airman's civilian employment (part time, full time, not employed).

Because this was a survey of spouses, it did not include active-duty airmen who are single parents. These airmen may also face challenges related to child care, child well-being, finances, and deployments. This subpopulation is relatively rare in the Air Force, however: About 1 percent of the enlisted force and less than 1 percent (0.003) of the office corps are single with dependents in the household (dependents may include adults as well) (AFPC, 2010). Thus, a survey would be unlikely to capture enough of these 2,747 airmen to enable separate analysis unless a concerted effort was made to identify and recruit single parents.

Making Sense of the Survey Results

To help enhance Air Force family support efforts, we developed policy options aimed at the most commonly reported problems and the factors associated with them that we think are worth exploring. The survey focused on the associated factors that our research sponsor, AF/A1, manages programs to address, rather than on such factors as poor health, which the Office of the Air Force Surgeon General would address. Also, the survey section on problems did not ask whether spouses thought the Air Force should help them solve their problems or whether they would want the Air Force to help.

Some apparent problems require further inquiry. Why do so few spouses attend deployment briefings? Why are some dissatisfied with deployment support services? Why are enlisted spouses more likely than officers' spouses to report problems finding activities for children after school and on weekends? We understand that part of the Year of the Air Force Family activities included focus groups with family members: These survey results spotlighted some areas worthy of pursuit in such a qualitative forum.

---

[1] Recall that 22 percent of dual-military active-duty Air Force officers and 9 percent of dual-military active-duty Air Force enlisted personnel are married to a member of the Air National Guard or Air Force Reserve.

Although our recommendations focus on the most commonly reported problems, it would be erroneous to assume that programs addressing issues that were least problematic should be cut. These programs may well be the reason these areas are the least problematic. For example, Air Force school liaison officers might be the reason parents were least likely to report that they had trouble getting assistance communicating with schools, managing home schooling, or enrolling in public or private school. Cutting that program might actually elevate these issues to the level of problematic for more Air Force families.

Overall, we found that spouses of active-duty airmen are satisfied with their lives and with life in the Air Force, and that did not vary significantly for any of the key subgroups we examined: officer and enlisted, dual-military and civilian spouses, residence on or off base, or parents and nonparents. More than 90 percent were satisfied with the well-being of their family, nearly that many were satisfied with their own life, and more than 80 percent were satisfied with Air Force family life. The most recent DMDC survey of active-duty spouses from all services, conducted in 2006, found that 61 percent rated themselves as satisfied or very satisfied with the military way of life (23 percent were neither satisfied nor dissatisfied and 16 percent were dissatisfied or very dissatisfied) (DMDC, 2007). As a rough comparison, in an aggregate of Gallup polls conducted prior to our survey, 88 percent of married Americans reported being very or somewhat satisfied with their own personal lives (Carroll, 2007).[2]

We could say that the Air Force spouse population is so satisfied that the Air Force does not need to take any additional action to improve spouse and family well-being. But spouse satisfaction is not the only goal the organization targets. The fewer problems that families are having, the more airmen are available to focus on their duties while at work and the less likely they are to have to take time off to accommodate family problems, such as limited child care. Furthermore, the Air Force is dedicated to continuous improvement and wants to be able to continue to attract and retain high-quality airmen. Airmen whose spouses have been dissatisfied with Air Force life may have already left the service, so their experiences are not captured in this study.

Recommendations

Our findings suggest several courses of action the Air Force could take to provide additional support to Air Force families.

Offer Airmen Options that Minimize Geographic Relocation, When Possible, and Expand Support to Families During the PCS Process

Families may prefer to stabilize geographically during particular points in their children's lives (e.g., middle of high school) or during a spouse's career development. Although the Air Force may have the most geographically stable families of the military services, any additional room to provide families options for greater stability would be beneficial.[3]

---

[2]   A caveat to the comparison: In addition to the different wording of the Gallup survey item, the population of military spouses is more likely to be female and younger than the average married American and, by definition, is more likely to have a spouse employed full-time rather than part-time or not employed.

[3]   Active-duty Air Force members surveyed in August 2009 reported an average of 20.9 months since their last PCS, compared to 16.9 months for their peers in the Navy, 14.6 months for the Army, and 10.7 months—or about one-half that of the Air Force—for the Marine Corps (DMDC, 2010, p. 108).

One example of a program to assist with stabilization that the Air Force has had in place since the beginning of 2004 is the High School Seniors Assignment Deferment Program (U.S. Air Force, 2004). This program allows enlisted airmen up through the rank of senior master sergeant and officers through the rank of lieutenant colonel to defer relocation for a year if their child is entering the senior year of high school. When compatible with the Air Force mission, the Air Force should support programs like this to account for family preferences in the assignment process.

We recommend the Air Force also focus on expanding support to families during the PCS moving process, an experience that may be more common among Air Force families than deployments. Some families enjoy the opportunity to live in different parts of the country or overseas or are unhappy with a particular assignment and welcome the opportunity to relocate. And some such moves will likely be needed across the course of an Air Force career, regardless. Whether moving is desired or not, families may need assistance with associated problems.

Relocation can present a myriad of challenges to Air Force families. It may require a new job search for civilian spouses. A dip in family income may result from an employment gap, loss of seniority or eligibility for benefits, or the inability to find a job that offers pay and/or hours comparable to the spouse's job at the previous location. Previous research has indicated that geographic relocation affects the employment status and income of military spouses negatively (Cooney, Segal, and De Angelis, 2009; Castaneda and Harrell, 2008). Additionally, a homeowner who has not been able to sell a home at the previous location may have to continue to pay that mortgage while also paying for housing at the new location. For parents, a new town can require a search for quality schools and day care. School-aged children may face classes significantly ahead or behind the pace of their previous instruction, credits that do not translate, and/or different graduation requirements, as well as the need to make new friends and more.

This survey did not cover the full range of PCS problems a family might encounter (e.g., the effects on families' social support networks, damage or loss of personal property during the move), so the need for PCS support and assistance may extend beyond additional attention to the domains of spousal employment and child-related issues.

Expand the Availability of Air Force Child Care

New Air Force initiatives may resolve some of the child-care problems existing at the time of this survey. In July 2010, the Air Force Chief of Staff broadcast his commitment to "add sufficient capacity to our child development centers to eliminate the child-care space deficit by the end of FY12" (Schwartz, 2010).

Further expanding the availability of child care could help spouses, particularly dual-military spouses, balance their child-care needs with their work schedules. About one-half of dual-military spouses reported that their work schedule and/or the hours Air Force child care is available are related to their child-care problems. Additionally, across all spouses, about 40 percent with an employment problem and more than 20 percent with a child-related problem associated their problems finding child care available at the right hours. The Air Force may need to extend the hours some child care is available, or increase the number of slots in certain time periods to meet the demand. Wait lists may provide some indication of demand, although some spouses may not bother to sign up for already lengthy wait lists.

To ensure that the needs of dual-military parents are met, improvements should include ensuring sufficient resources so that child care is available during hours that military personnel must work and that sufficient extended child-care is available to account for unexpectedly lengthy work weeks or irregular shifts.

Offer More and/or Better Publicize After-School and Weekend Youth Activities

Parents' survey responses suggest that the Air Force should consider offering more youth activities after school and on weekends, and/or better publicize the existing programs. These programs can supplement child care, but they can also help develop children's skills and social networks outside of school. Additionally, a study on adolescents in Army families suggests that participation in these kinds of activities, particularly sports, can help to reduce child stress during parent deployments (Wong and Gerras, 2010).

Ensure Recreational Programming Meets the Full Range of Interests Among Military Families, Including Nonathletic Activities

The Air Force appears to do quite well in providing facilities and programming to support the physical fitness and outdoor activities of its married population. Approximately 20 percent of our surveyed spouses, however, indicated that in the past year, they or a family member participated in arts and crafts only off base. Furthermore, 15 percent of parents who reported a child-related problem identified "the kinds of activities offered by Air Force youth programs" as a factor. The Air Force may need to improve marketing or availability of its nonathletic activities and to assess whether its current offerings match the interests of Air Force spouses and families.

The Craft and Hobby Association (CHA) estimates the U.S. craft and hobby industry at $27.4 billion, and crafting has remained strong during the economic recession (CHA, 2010). Based on the association's 2009 U.S. annual attitude and usage survey, the key motivating factors people reported for crafting were

1. a sense of accomplishment
2. relaxation
3. memory keeping
4. health
5. economy and value
6. recommendations by friends or family
7. enables time to spend with others
8. interaction with children (CHA, 2010).

The CHA's identification of flourishing craft and hobby markets in the United States can suggest which activities might have a wide appeal. Their survey shows that top ten craft segments are

1. scrapbooking and memory crafts
2. home décor painting and accessorizing/finishing
3. woodworking
4. cake decorating
5. art and drawing
6. jewelry making
7. card making
8. floral arranging

9. quilting
10. crocheting (CHA, 2010).

In addition to arts and crafts, other activities that may interest families, contribute to their welfare, and warrant greater Air Force sponsorship include gardening, cooking, singing, dancing, acting, playing musical instruments, caring for pets, collecting, and reading and book clubs.

The Air Force should offer a wide range of activities to meet the needs of Air Force families with members who are uninterested or unable to participate in highly physical activities. Craft and hobby workshops, classes, exhibits, competitions, and performances can help families bond, develop skills and confidence in children and adults, provide opportunities to build friendships and social support networks, and promote healthy forms of relaxation and stress relief.

Deepen Support to Families Experiencing Deployments

Deepening support to families with a deployed airman, whether through increasing awareness of what is already available or adding to existing efforts, may help alleviate some of the problems that Air Force families typically face during a deployment cycle. Particularly since many airmen do not deploy with a unit, meaning that unit-based deployment briefings and support activities do not make sense, directed outreach to families as soon as their airmen are selected for deployment may be advantageous. The Air Force already provides a number of avenues to help families during deployments or to facilitate reintegration afterward (e.g., child-care options). It is possible that additional resourcing for or awareness of these programs would advance the cause. Also, since about one-half of civilian spouses reported that their employment-related problems worsened during their spouse's latest deployment, the Air Force should ensure that deployment support addresses the associated employment-related needs.

Increase Awareness of Financial and Employment Programs and Services

It may be that an increase in publicity about the offerings of Air Force Financial Education and Spouse Employment Assistance programs will reduce the number of spouses who believe that Air Force programs do not address their specific types of problems, but the Air Force should also explore whether there are other gaps that it could address as well. Civilian spouses and spouses with children appear to need this most, so outreach and information-gathering efforts should include a focus on those populations.

"Inconvenient access" to Air Force services mentioned in this survey could mean a number of things: that the spouse lives too far away, that assistance is offered when the spouse must work, that the spouse is unable to obtain trustworthy short-term child care to be able to attend classes, that the spouse cannot attend classes or visit during available hours because the family only has one car and that is the one the airman takes to work, etc. Since email and websites are a preferred means of receiving information, options such as webinars, posting online educational modules, or financial advice chat rooms where spouses can directly query a financial expert could be popular.

Improve Employment Opportunities for Civilian Spouses

Employment assistance in the form of job-seeking advice is of limited value to spouses facing a lack of job openings or career opportunities in their area. We echo our colleagues' recommendations for the services to take a more-active role in providing employer incentives for hiring military spouses and to look at the extent to which contracted jobs on military bases could be filled by military spouses or to which incentives could be used to encourage contractors to hire military spouses (Castaneda and Harrell, 2008; Harrell et al., 2004). The Army Spouse Employment Partnership Program offers one possible model for partnering with private-sector and federal-government employers to increase employment and career opportunities for spouses. That program has engaged 31 Fortune 100 and Fortune 500 companies and two military agencies to address the needs of Army spouses through modifications of their hiring processes and "creating employment continuity programs and career portability with no loss in tenure or benefits" (U.S. Army, 2010). Finally, the Air Force could lobby more states to deem military spouses eligible for unemployment benefits if they left their previous job to follow their military spouse to a new assignment.[4]

Focus Communication on Preferred Electronic Methods and Air Force Publications

In this survey, spouses indicated that the best ways to increase their awareness of and supply information about Air Force programs were through email, websites, newsletters, and newspapers. Although other modes may be useful to reach a minority of spouses, these preferences provide some indication of where the Air Force could focus its communication efforts. These channels could be used to share information about new policies and programs; introduce modifications to existing programs, such as the name change of the Family Support Center to Airman and Family Readiness Center; and selectively reach out to certain populations, such as families about to move or experience a deployment.

Ask Airmen to Provide Spouse Contact Information and Maintain that Information in the Administrative Personnel Files

To facilitate communication with spouses, the Air Force should create fields to store telephone and email contact information in personnel records so that it can be readily used to contact spouses directly. Nearly 50 percent of spouses said their preferred means of communication about Air Force programs and services is email, yet the Air Force administrative files retain no email addresses for airmen's spouses. A space for an airman's "home phone" is provided, but in an era of increasing cell phone ownership and decreasing landlines at home, we can no longer assume that the home telephone number listed for an airman is a direct line to the spouse. Also, the home telephone number or address for an airman might not be the same as for his or her spouse, such as when the airman is serving unaccompanied overseas tour or single-year tour at a professional military school. As with a "do not call" registry, the Air Force might want to give spouses the option not to receive contact from the Air Force for anything but an emergency, but at least in the case of an emergency, the Air Force would have a direct line to the spouse.

Conclusion

The problems that Air Force families face are not unique. Work-family balance issues and financial worries plague many families in the United States. Recognizing that force readiness

---

[4] For a table of each state's unemployment benefit eligibility regarding married people and/or military spouses who leave their job to relocate with their spouse, see Morton, 2010.

is multifaceted, the Air Force has made family well-being a priority. Despite some room for improvement, the results presented in this report have highlighted areas where the Air Force, and its families, is already doing well. Further, it has also pointed out areas where additional improvements may have the greatest positive impact on Air Force families, and thus, on the overall ability of the Air Force to accomplish its mission.

Air Force Spouse Survey Instrument

Introduction and Human Subjects Protection Section

Work Phone Version Only—Otherwise Start at "Hello"

May I please speak to [read-in name from sample/or updated name]?

Hello. My name is _____. I am calling from Abt-SRBI on behalf of the Air Force. I'm conducting a short, 15–20 minute survey on what spouses of Air Force military personnel think about the Air Force leadership and programs or services the Air Force offers. The Air Force will use the results of the survey to make potential changes to various programs and services.

Cell Phone Version Only—Otherwise Start With S1.

> **CATI: Read Offer Only If Up2 = 2.**
> **Or Cell Phone Version S1 = 2. Cell Phone Spouse.**

We'd appreciate the opportunity to include your opinions and if you qualify for the survey we'd like to send you $10 for your time.

> C1. If you are now driving or doing any activity requiring your full attention, I need to call you back later. Are you able to talk now?
>
> 1. Yes—**Go to S1**
> 2. No—**Set up callback—offer toll free number**
> 9. Hard refusal
>
> **Interviewer: If respondent says it is not a good time, try to arrange a callback. Offer toll-free number they can use to call back to complete the survey.**

Work Phone Version Only—Otherwise Start with S1.

> W1. Your household has been randomly selected to participate in this study. Would you be willing to provide us with the name and phone number of your spouse so we can ask [her/him] to participate in this very important research study?
>
> 1. Yes, willing to give spouse's name and number—**go to UP1**
> 2. Not willing to give spouse's number—**screen out; W1 refused spouse's number**

3. Unable to talk—**schedule callback**
4. No spouse/not married—**screen out W1 no spouse**
5. Not an Air Force household—**screen out W1 not AF HH.**
9. Hard refusal

S1.   Today we are speaking with the spouses of Air Force service members. Are you or may I speak to a person married to someone in the Air Force?

1. Yes I am—**continue to intro before S2.**
2. Coming to the phone repeat intro and S1.
3. Set up callback at same number.
4. Set up callback at different number—**Go to UP1.**
5. No service member spouse—**end call; screen out S1 no AF spouse.**
6. Not an Air Force HH—**screen out; S1 not AF HH.**
8. Soft refusal—**end call; not called back if cell phone version.**
9. Hard refusal—**end call.**

Qualified Level 1: S1 = 1

UP1. **Interviewer: update respondent's information**

1. Update phone
2. Update name
3. Update name and phone

UP2. **interviewer: record if new number is a landline or cell phone**

Is that a landline or cell phone?

1. Landline—**set up callback**
2. Cell phone—**terminate call—interviewer dispo as cell phone callback**

CATI: Change text of "Foreign Language—Russian" dispo to "Cell Phone Callback"
CATI: IF UP2 = 2, respondent should get all "CELL PHONE VERSION ONLY" questions
CATI VARIABLE: 1 = Cell phone—start callback at cell phone intro

If Cell Phone Version and S1 = 1

We'd appreciate the opportunity to include your opinions and if you qualify for the survey we'd like to send you $10 for your time.

Okay, first I'd like to let you know that the Air Force has commissioned the RAND Corporation, a non-profit research company, to analyze the survey results. RAND will use the information you provide for research purposes only and will protect the confidentiality of this information. They will not disclose your identity to anyone, except as required by law, and will destroy all information that identifies you at the end of the study. You do not have to take part in this survey and you can stop at any time without giving a reason. You can skip any questions you don't want to answer. If you do not know the answer it's also okay to say that.

Interviewer: In general, do not offer response options of 8 "Don't Know" and 9 "Refused." Use only if the respondent indicates that he or she does not wish to answer or does not have an answer.

Before we begin, do you have any questions about the survey?

Interviewer: Read the following if necessary:

If you have any questions about the interview itself, you may contact

[Abt SRBI name and contact information]
RAND Survey Contact [name and contact information]
RAND Human Subjects Protection Committee [name and contact information]

S2.   We are only permitted to survey adults aged 18 years or older. Are you 18 years old or older?

1. Yes
2. No—end call; screen out S2—not 18+
9. (vol.) Refused—end call; screen out S2 ref 18+

Demographics

First I'm going to ask you some questions about you and your current spouse in the Air Force.

1.   Do you currently live on or off base?

1. On
2. Off
9. (vol.) Refused

2.   **If "Off" on number 1:**
   How far away from the base do you live?

   Read options below
1. Less than 30 minutes.
2. 30 minutes or more.
9. (vol.) Refused

3.   Are you currently living in the continental United States? [United States, not including Alaska and Hawaii]

1. Yes
2. No
9. (vol.) Refused

4.   **Record by observation—ask only if necessary:**
   What is your gender?

1. Male
2. Female
9. (vol.) Refused

5.   What is the highest degree or level of school that you have completed?

   Read options below
   1. 12 years of school or less, no diploma or GED
   2. High school diploma or GED
   3. Some college or trade school, but no degree
   4. Associate's degree or trade school equivalent
   5. Bachelor's degree or equivalent
   6. Graduate degree
   9. (vol.) Refused

6.   Are you currently employed full time, part time, or are you not employed at this time?

   1. Yes—Full Time
   2. Yes—Part Time
   3. Not employed at this time
   9. (vol.) Refused

7.   Are you currently in school full time, part time, or are you not in school at this time?

   1. Yes—Full Time
   2. Yes—Part Time
   3. Not in school at this time
   9. (vol.) Refused

8.   How old are you?

   _____ Age in Years (range 18–98)
   9. (vol.) Refused

9.   How many children under the age of 6 live with you at least half of the time?

   _____ Number (range 0–8, 8 = 8+)
   9. (vol.) Refused

10.   How many children between the age of 6 and 18 live with you at least half of the time?

   _____ Number (range 0–8, 8 = 8+)
   9. (vol.) Refused

11.   Do you have any children over the age of 18 who live with you at least half of the time?

   1. Yes
   2. No
   9. (vol.) Refused

12.   Do you or does anyone living with you at least half of the time receive special education or early intervention services, or are any of them in the Exceptional Family Member Program (EFMP)?

   1. Yes
   2. No—Skip to Q13.
   8. (vol.) Don't Know—Skip to Q13
   9. (vol.) Refused—Skip to Q13

12a.   Would that be . . .

Read list—record multiples:

1. You
2. One or more children under the age of 18
3. One or more children or other relatives over the age of 18
8. (vol.) Don't Know
9. (vol.) Refused

Qualified Level 2: After Q12a

Deployment

Now we would like to ask you some questions about deployment.

13. If you are in the military, were you deployed for more than 30 days in the past 2 years?

1. Yes, I'm in the military and I was deployed for more than 30 days in the past 2 years.
2. No, I'm in the military but I have not been deployed for more than 30 days in the past 2 years
3. No, I'm not in the military.
8. (vol.) Don't Know
9. (vol.) Refused

14. Was your spouse deployed for more than 30 days in the past 2 years?

1. Yes
2. No—**Skip to Q17**.
8. (vol.) Don't Know—**Skip to Q17**
9. (vol.) Refused—**Skip to Q17**

15. **If Q14 = 1 else skip to Q17:**
     Did you attend any deployment briefings at any time before, during, or right after your spouse's last deployment?

1. Yes
2. No
8. (vol.) Don't Know
9. (vol.) Refused

16. Overall, how would you rate the services provided to your family to meet their needs during your spouse's last deployment?

Read options below
1. Excellent
2. Good
3. Average
4. Fair
5. Poor
8. (vol.) Don't Know/Was not offered any services
9. (vol.) Refused

Child Problems

If number 9 or number 10 = 1–8, else skip to Q20:
Now we would like to know more about your family life.

17.   In particular, we would like to know about any difficulties you may have experienced regarding the children under the age of 18 who live with you at least half time. Please indicate whether you have experienced any of the following problems related to any child of yours in the past year.

Read options below

17a.   Obtaining child care while you work or attend school.
1.   Yes
2.   No
8.   (vol.) Don't Know
9.   (vol.) Refused

17b.   Obtaining child care so you can get other things accomplished or take care of yourself or people other than your children
1.   Yes
2.   No
8.   (vol.) Don't Know
9.   (vol.) Refused

17c.   Your child's academic performance in school
1.   Yes
2.   No
8.   (vol.) Don't Know
9.   (vol.) Refused

In the past year, have you had difficulties with…

17d.   A child having emotional or behavioral problems
1.   Yes
2.   No
8.   (vol.) Don't Know
9.   (vol.) Refused

17e.   Finding activities to keep children safe or busy after school or on weekends
1.   Yes
2.   No
8.   (vol.) Don't Know
9.   (vol.) Refused

17f.   Finding activities to develop their skills outside of school
1.   Yes
2.   No
8.   (vol.) Don't Know

9. (vol.) Refused

In the past year, have you had difficulties with...

17g.   [If number 12 = 1 AND number 12a = 2] Managing a child's special needs, such as help with a physical disability or the need for special education
1. Yes
2. No
8. (vol.) Don't Know
9. (vol.) Refused

17h.   Getting help communicating with schools about issues like transferring schools, school records, graduation requirements, or extracurricular activity requirements
1. Yes
2. No
8. (vol.) Don't Know
9. (vol.) Refused

17i.   Getting assistance managing home schooling or enrollment in public or private school
1. Yes
2. No
8. (vol.) Don't Know
9. (vol.) Refused

18. **If Q17a–i all = 2, 8, 9 or Q14 = 2, 8, 9 and Q13 = 2, 3, 8, 9 skip to Q19:**
Overall, were the child-related problems you experienced worse or better during your or your spouse's last deployment? Were they...

Read options below
1. Much Worse
2. Somewhat Worse
3. No Difference
4. Somewhat Better
5. Much Better
8. (vol.) Don't Know
9. (vol.) Refused

19.   **If Q17a–i all = 2,8,9 skip to Q20:**
Please tell me if you think the child-related problems you had in the past year were related to…

Read options below (if necessary…"was that an issue related to the child-related problems you had in the past year?")

19b.   A recent move or PCS **(If needed, explain that PCS means permanent change of station or moving from one station to the next.)**
1. Yes
2. No
8. (vol.) Don't Know
9. (vol.) Refused

19c.   Your work schedule, if you worked in the past year
1. Yes
2. No
3. (vol.) did not work
8. (vol.) Don't Know
9. (vol.) Refused

19d.   The hours Air Force child care is available
1. Yes
2. No
8. (vol.) Don't Know
9. (vol.) Refused

Were your child-related problems related to…

19e.   The distance between your work and Air Force child care, if you worked in the past year
1. Yes
2. No
     (vol.) did not work
8. (vol.) Don't Know
9. (vol.) Refused

19f.   The distance between Air Force after school activities or programs and your child's school
1. Yes
2. No
8. (vol.) Don't Know
9. (vol.) Refused

19g.   The kinds of activities offered by Air Force youth programs
1. Yes
2. No
8. (vol.) Don't Know
9. (vol.) Refused

Were your child-related problems related to…

19h.   The inability of Air Force programs to help you manage your child's educational issues
1. Yes
2. No
8. (vol.) Don't Know
9. (vol.) Refused

Financial Problems

20. Now we would like to ask you about your financial situation. Please indicate whether you had any of the following financial problems in the past year.

Read options below

Did you have problems with…

20a.   Foreclosure on a home
1. Yes
2. No
8. (vol.) Don't Know
9. (vol.) Refused

20b.   Trouble paying debt, bills, or mortgage
1. Yes
2. No
8. (vol.) Don't Know
9. (vol.) Refused

20c.   Bankruptcy
1. Yes
2. No
8. (vol.) Don't Know
9. (vol.) Refused

20d.   Inability to save **(If respondent asks, this refers to saving money.)**
1. Yes
2. No
8. (vol.) Don't Know
9. (vol.) Refused

21.   **If all number 20a–d = 2, 8, 9 or Q14 = 2, 8, 9 AND Q13 = 2, 3, 8, 9 skip to Q22:**
Overall, were the financial problems you experienced worse or better during your or your spouse's last deployment? Were they…

Read options below
1.   Much Worse
2.   Somewhat Worse
3.   No Difference
4.   Somewhat Better
5.   Much Better
8.   (vol.) Don't Know
9.   (vol.) Refused

22.   **If all number 20a–d = 2, 8, 9 skip to Q23:**
Please tell me if you think any of the following issues are related to the financial problems you had in the past year.

Read options below (If necessary…"was that an issue related to the financial problems you had in the past year?")

Were your financial problems related to…

22b.   A recent move or PCS **(If needed, explain that PCS means permanent change of station or moving from one station to the next.)**
1.   Yes
2.   No
8.   (vol.) Don't Know
9.   (vol.) Refused

22c.   Your employment status
1.   Yes
2.   No
8.   (vol.) Don't Know
9.   (vol.) Refused

22d.   **If number 9 OR number 10 = 1-8 else skip to Q22e:**
The costs related to raising children
1.   Yes
2.   No
8.   (vol.) Don't Know
9.   (vol.) Refused

Were your financial problems related to…

22e. The inability of Air Force financial education programs to address the kinds of problems you have.
1.   Yes
2.   No
8.   (vol.) Don't Know
9.   (vol.) Refused

22f. Inconvenient access to Air Force financial education programs
1. Yes
2. No
8. (vol.) Don't Know
9. (vol.) Refused

22g. Lack of information about Air Force financial education programs
1. Yes
2. No
8. (vol.) Don't Know
9. (vol.) Refused

Qualified Level 3: After Q22g

Employment Problems

23. **If number 6 = 1 "yes—full time" or 2 "yes—part time":**
    Now we would like to ask about your employment situation. I am going to list a number of reasons why people work. More than one of these may apply to you, but at the end of the list, I'd like you to please tell me the main reason why you work. **(Record only one.)**

    1. To provide half or more of the income for your family
    2. To supplement your spouse's income so you can cover your basic living expenses
    3. To supplement your spouse's income so you can afford some of the nicer things in life
    4. For the personal satisfaction of working or pursuing a career
    5. To keep from getting bored
    6. (vol.) Other/none of the above
    8. (vol.) Don't Know
    9. (vol.) Refused

24. Please indicate whether you have had any of the following problems related to your employment situation in the past year.

    Read options below

    Have you had problems in the past year with…

    24a.   Finding a job in general
    1. Yes
    2. No
    8. (vol.) Don't Know
    9. (vol.) Refused

    24b.   Finding a job that matches your education, abilities or interests
    1. Yes
    2. No
    8. (vol.) Don't Know
    9. (vol.) Refused

24c. Being able to work the number of hours you want or the schedule you want, If you worked in the past year,
1. Yes
2. No
3. (vol.) did not work
8. (vol.) Don't Know
9. (vol.) Refused

24d. Being able to get any additional education or training necessary for your career development
1. Yes
2. No
8. (vol.) Don't Know
9. (vol.) Refused

25. **If number 24 a–d all = 2, 8, 9 or Q14 = 2, 8, 9 and Q13 = 2, 3, 8, 9 skip to Q26:**
Overall, were the employment problems you experienced worse or better during your or your spouse's last deployment? Were they…

Read options below
1. Much Worse
2. Somewhat Worse
3. No Difference
4. Somewhat Better
5. Much Better
8. (vol.) Don't Know
9. (vol.) Refused

26. **If number 24a–d all = 2, 8, 9 skip to Q27:**
Please tell me if you think any of the following issues are related to the employment problems you have had in the past year.

Read options below (If necessary.….was that an issue related to the employment problems you have had in the past year?)

Were your employment problems related to…

26b. A recent move or PCS
1. Yes
2. No
8. (vol.) Don't Know
9. (vol.) Refused

26c. **If number 9 or number 10 = 1–8 else skip to Q26d:**
Finding child care that will match the hours you need to work
1. Yes
2. No
8. (vol.) Don't Know
9. (vol.) Refused

26d.   Lack of information about Air Force employment assistance programs
1. Yes
2. No
8. (vol.) Don't Know
9. (vol.) Refused

Were your employment problems related to…

26e.   The inability of Air Force employment assistance programs to address the kinds of employment problems you have had
1. Yes
2. No
8. (vol.) Don't Know
9. (vol.) Refused

26f.   Inconvenient access to Air Force employment assistance programs
1. Yes
2. No
8. (vol.) Don't Know
9. (vol.) Refused

26g.   **If number 9 or number 10 = 1–8 else skip to Q27:**
Finding a job that pays enough to cover the cost of child care while you are working
1. Yes
2. No
8. (vol.) Don't Know
9. (vol.) Refused

Recreation

Now we would like to ask you about the leisure activities that you and your family did together in the past year.

27.   How satisfied are you with the amount of leisure time your family spent together, in the past year?

Read options below
1. Very Satisfied
2. Somewhat Satisfied
3. Neither Satisfied nor Dissatisfied
4. Somewhat Dissatisfied
5. Very Satisfied
8. (vol.) Don't Know
9. (vol.) Refused

Did you or your family participate in any of the following leisure activities on or off base in the past year? I will read an activity and you can indicate whether or not your family participated in it, and if so, whether it was on base, off base, or both on and off base.

28.   Did anyone in your family participate in events coordinated by the Officers' Club, NCO club or Enlisted Club? **[If needed, NCO = noncommissioned officer]**

1.   Yes
2.   No
8.   (vol.) Don't Know
9.   (vol.) Refused

29.   **If "yes" on number 28:**
Did you or your family do this on base, off base, or both?

1.   On Base
2.   Off Base
3.   Both On and Off Base
8.   (vol.) Don't Know
9.   (vol.) Refused

30. Did anyone in your family use resources at a local library?

1.   Yes
2.   No
8.   (vol.) Don't Know
9.   (vol.) Refused

31.   **If "yes" on number 30:**
Did you or your family use a library on base, off base, or both?

1.   On Base
2.   Off Base
3.   Both On and Off Base
8.   (vol.) Don't Know
9.   (vol.) Refused

In the past year,

32.   Did anyone in your family use a local gym or fitness center?

1.   Yes
2.   No
8.   (vol.) Don't Know
9.   (vol.) Refused

33.   **If "yes" on number 32:**
Did you or your family use a gym or fitness center on base, off base, or both?

1.   On Base
2.   Off Base
3.   Both On and Off Base
8.   (vol.) Don't Know
9.   (vol.) Refused

34. Did anyone in your family participate in outdoor recreation activities?

   1. Yes
   2. No
   8. (vol.) Don't Know
   9. (vol.) Refused

35. **If "yes" on number 34:**
   Did you or your family participate in outdoor recreation activities on base, off base, or both?

   1. On Base
   2. Off Base
   3. Both On and Off Base
   8. (vol.) Don't Know
   9. (vol.) Refused

In the past year,

36. Did anyone in your family do arts and crafts projects with other people?

   1. Yes
   2. No
   8. (vol.) Don't Know
   9. (vol.) Refused

37. **If "yes" on number 36:**
   Did you or your family do arts and crafts projects with other people on base, off base, or both?

   1. On Base
   2. Off Base
   3. Both On and Off Base
   8. (vol.) Don't Know
   9. (vol.) Refused

38. Did anyone in your family use the Auto Hobby shops to work on cars or learn how to work on them?

   1. Yes
   2. No
   8. (vol.) Don't Know
   9. (vol.) Refused

39. **If "yes" on number 38:**
   Did you or your family do this on base, off base, or both?

   1. On Base
   2. Off Base
   3. Both On and Off Base
   8. (vol.) Don't Know
   9. (vol.) Refused

In the past year,

40.   Did anyone in your family purchase event tickets or make tour or travel reservations?

   1. Yes
   2. No
   8. (vol.) Don't Know
   9. (vol.) Refused

41.   **If "yes" on number 40:**
       For purchasing event or travel tickets, did you use ticket or travel services located on base, off base, or both?

   1. On Base
   2. Off Base
   3. Both On and Off Base
   8. (vol.) Don't Know
   9. (vol.) Refused

42.   Did anyone in your family play golf?

   1. Yes
   2. No
   8. (vol.) Don't Know
   9. (vol.) Refused

43.   **If "yes" on number 42:**
       Did you or your family play golf on base, off base, or both?

   1. On Base
   2. Off Base
   3. Both On and Off Base
   8. (vol.) Don't Know
   9. (vol.) Refused

In the past year,

44.   Did anyone in your family go bowling?

   1. Yes
   2. No
   8. (vol.) Don't Know
   9. (vol.) Refused

45.   **[If "yes" on number 44:**
       id you or you family go bowling on base, off base, or both?

   1. On Base
   2. Off Base
   3. Both On and Off Base
   8. (vol.) Don't Know
   9. (vol.) Refused

46. Did anyone in your family participate in activities at a community center?

    1. Yes
    2. No
    8. (vol.) Don't Know
    9. (vol.) Refused

47. **If "yes" on number 46:**
    Did you or your family go to a community center on base, off base, or both?

    1. On Base
    2. Off Base
    3. Both On and Off Base
    8. (vol.) Don't Know
    9. (vol.) Refused

Qualified Level 4: After Q47

Overall Assessments and Attitudes Toward the Air Force

Okay, now I'm going to ask you about some more general Air Force programs and services.

48. Did you realize that the name of the Family Support Center was changed to the Airman and Family Readiness Center in the past year?

    1. Yes
    2. No
    8. (vol.) Don't Know
    9. (vol.) Refused

49. **If "yes" on number 48, else skip to Q51:**
    Did you find the name change to be confusing or misleading?

    1. Yes
    2. No
    8. (vol.) Don't Know
    9. (vol.) Refused

50. **[If "yes" on number 48, else skip to Q51:**
    Did the name change cause you problems in finding family support types of services?

    1. Yes, it caused me problems.
    2. No, it did not cause me any problems with finding services.
    8. (vol.) Don't Know
    9. (vol.) Refused

51.   What are your two most preferred ways of learning about Air Force programs and services? I'm going to read a list of options and when I am done, please tell me which are your two most preferred ways.

Read options below

Prompt for two responses but allow only one if that's all they want to give. Reread options if necessary. CATI accepts up to 2 answer codes 1–8 or code 9 with or without codes 1–8. Only allow one with code 98 or 99.

1. Air Force web sites
2. Air Force newsletters or newspapers
3. Posters or flyers on base
4. Telephone calls from someone on base
5. Emails from the Air Force
6. Talking in person with someone at the base
7. Social networking tools like Facebook, MySpace, Twitter
8. Receiving information through mail
9. (vol.) NO (OTHER) WAYS ON LIST
98. (vol.) Don't Know
99. (vol.) Refused

Now we want to finish by asking you some questions about Air Force life and Air Force leadership. Please indicate how much you agree or disagree with the following statements.

52.   Overall, I am satisfied with my life today. Do you…?

Read options below

1. Strongly Agree
2. Somewhat Agree
3. Neither Agree nor Disagree
4. Somewhat Disagree
5. Strongly Disagree
8. (vol.) Don't Know
9. (vol.) Refused

53.   Overall, I am satisfied with the level of well-being of my family today. Do you…?

Read options below

1. Strongly Agree
2. Somewhat Agree
3. Neither Agree nor Disagree
4. Somewhat Disagree
5. Strongly Disagree
8. (vol.) Don't Know
9. (vol.) Refused

54.   My spouse's supervisor cares about our family's well-being. Do you...?

Read options below

1.   Strongly Agree
2.   Somewhat Agree
3.   Neither Agree nor Disagree
4.   Somewhat Disagree
5.   Strongly Disagree
8.   (vol.) Don't Know
9.   (vol.) Refused

55.   My spouse's squadron or unit commander or commander equivalent cares about our family's well being. Do you...?

Read options below

1.   Strongly Agree
2.   Somewhat Agree
3.   Neither Agree nor Disagree
4.   Somewhat Disagree
5.   Strongly Disagree
8.   (vol.) Don't Know
9.   (vol.) Refused

56.   Senior leaders at the very top of the Air Force, in Washington, D.C., care about the well-being of Air Force families. Do you...?

Read options below

1.   Strongly Agree
2.   Somewhat Agree
3.   Neither Agree nor Disagree
4.   Somewhat Disagree
5.   Strongly Disagree
8.   (vol.) Don't Know
9.   (vol.) Refused

57.   Families receive more support the first time a spouse is deployed compared to later deployments. Do you...?

Read options below

1.   Strongly Agree
2.   Somewhat Agree
3.   Neither Agree nor Disagree
4.   Somewhat Disagree
5.   Strongly Disagree
8.   (vol.) Don't Know
9.   (vol.) Refused

58.   Overall I am satisfied with Air Force family life. Do you...?

Read options below

1.   Strongly Agree
2.   Somewhat Agree
3.   Neither Agree nor Disagree
4.   Somewhat Disagree

    5. Strongly Disagree
    8. (vol.) Don't Know
    9. (vol.) Refused

59.   How likely is it that your family will stay with the Air Force for another tour of duty?

    1. Very likely
    2. Somewhat likely
    3. Neither likely nor unlikely
    4. Somewhat unlikely
    5. Very unlikely
    8. (vol.) Don't Know
    9. (vol.) Refused

The survey is now complete. Thank you so much for taking the time to answer our questions!

[CELL VERSION AND S1 = 1 OR UP2 = 2 ONLY]:

C60. Before you go I would like to get your name and address to send you $10 for your time. May I have your name and an address where we can send you the money? (IF NECESSARY: Your name and address will never be associated with this survey it is only used to send you $10.)

    1. gave mailing address, record name, address, apt number, city, state, zip code.
    2. (vol.) respondent refuses/does not want the money.

Calculation of Response and Cooperation Rates

The American Association for Public Opinion Research (AAPOR) defines *response rate* as "the number of complete interviews with reporting units divided by the number of eligible reporting units in the sample" (2009, p. 35). We report AAPOR Response Rate 3 (RR3), which includes an estimate of the "proportion of cases of unknown eligibility is actually eligible" (AAPOR, 2009, p. 36). Our calculations use the proportional allocation (Council of American Survey Research Organizations) method of estimating the proportion of cases of unknown eligibility that is actually eligible. Smith (2009, p. 3) states that this method "has the advantages of being easily calculated from information readily available from each individual survey and being conservative (i.e., producing a high estimate of the eligibility rate and thereby not inflating the estimated response rate)." See Table B.1.

Estimates of the response rate for this telephone survey were somewhat complicated by the contents of the notification letter that was sent to prospective respondents. The letter was sent to a total of 2,936 individuals. The notification letter invited individuals to contact the survey center directly, if they wished, to take the survey or to schedule a time to take the survey. A total of 2,601 of the telephone numbers in the sample frame of 4,000 had contact with the survey center, either as a result of individuals initiating the call or as a result of the survey center initiating the call. However, the survey contractor did not identify who initiated the call.

We calculated the response rate twice, once using the number of telephone numbers contacted (Estimate 1) and once using the number of notification letters that were sent (Estimate 2). We used the same number of completes (802) for both calculations, but estimated the other components of the formula using the proportions found in the call data. For example, the proportion of refusals and break-offs among actual telephone contacts was 193 out of 2,601. We estimated the number of refusals and break-offs that would occur for a contact sample size of 2,936 as (193/2,601) x 2,936 = 217.

Our calculations for these two estimates of RR3 include calls screened out as if they were completed surveys. We also calculated two estimates of RR3 based only on completed surveys (i.e., not including screen-outs). Based on these calculations, the most conservative estimate of RR3 for this survey is 47 percent (assuming the number of contacts to be the number of notification letters sent out and not counting screen-outs as completes). Our upper bound estimate of RR3 for this survey is 49 percent (assuming the number of contacts to be the number of telephone numbers attempted and counting screen-outs as completes).

Similar calculations for AAPOR Cooperation Rate 3 yield a range of 77 to 81 percent.

Table B.1
Calculation of American Association of Public Opinion Research RR3

AAPOR Code	Formula	Estimate	
		1	2
Total phone numbers used		2,601	2,936
Completes and screen-outs (1.0/1.1)	I	919	934
Partial Interviews (1.2)	P	22	24
Refusal and break off (2.1)	R	193	217
Non Contact (2.2)	NC	107	120
Other (2.3)	O	37	41
Unknown household (3.1)	UH	42	47
Unknown other (3.2, 3.9)	UO	787	888
Not Eligible (4.0)	NE	494	557
e = Estimated proportion of cases of unknown eligibility that are eligible	$\dfrac{I+P+R+NC+O}{(I+P+R+NC+O)+NE}$	0.72	0.70
Response Rate 3	$\dfrac{I}{(I+P)+(R+NC+O)+e(UH+UO)}$	0.49	0.47

Construction of the Sample and of Sample Weights

Drawing the Sample

AFPC maintains personnel files for all Air Force personnel, and RAND Project Air Force regularly receives access to copies of these files to support its research for the Air Force in the manpower and personnel arena. The sample for this research project was drawn from the population of married active-duty Air Force personnel included in the April 2009 Air Force personnel files.

Married active-duty Air Force personnel can be identified as being married to another military member (either active duty or guard/reserve) or married to a civilian. The first row of Table C.1 sets out the numbers and distribution of this population as of April 2009.

From the populations shown in the first row, we drew random samples of the sizes shown in the second row. Because of their relatively smaller numbers among active-duty married personnel, officers and those married to another service member were oversampled. After the sample was drawn, the ordering of individuals within each of the four groups was randomized. Names, addresses, telephone numbers, and information identifying an individual's membership in one of the four groups shown here were provided to the survey contractor.

Weighting the Sample

The last row in Table C.1 shows the final sample sizes for completed telephone surveys. The sample was weighted to be representative of the entire population of married active-duty airmen.

Table C.1
Sample Selection: Air Force Population of Married Officers and Enlisted Airmen

	Officers Married to		Enlisted Married to		
	Service Members	Civilians	Service Members	Civilians	Total
Married Air Force active-duty population (number)	6,578	39,598	32,877	115,268	194,321
Sample provided to the survey contractor (number)	805	805	1,000	1,390	4,000
Final sample for Air Force spouse survey (number)	161	162	200	279	802

We weighted the responses to match the following airman population characteristics:

1. family
   a. officers married to service members
   b. officers married to civilians
   c. enlisted married to service members
   d. enlisted married to civilians
2. rank
   a. junior enlisted (airman basic, airman, airman first class, senior airman)
   b. senior enlisted (staff sergeant, technical sergeant, master sergeant, senior master sergeant, chief master sergeant)
   c. company-grade officer (second lieutenant, first lieutenant, captain)
   d. field-grade officer (major, lieutenant colonel, colonel)
3. children
   a. have children
   b. do not have children
4. race of the airman[1]
   a. white
   b. nonwhite.

A logistic regression with dummy variables for the above characteristics was used to estimate the probability that each of the 194,118 families in the population completed the survey:

$$\frac{I + P + R + NC + O}{(I + P + R + NC + O) + NE}$$

Weights were calculated as follows:

$$\frac{I}{(I + P) + (R + NC + O) + e(UH + UO)}$$

We completed data analyses using survey estimation procedures (StataCorp, 2007) to ensure appropriate estimates of standard errors.

---

[1] The personnel files do not indicate the race of the spouse.

Bibliography

AFPC—*See* Air Force Personnel Center.

Air Force Aid Society, "2009 Fact Sheet," 2010. As of September 29, 2010:
http://www.afas.org/About/FactSheet.cfm

Air Force Personnel Center, Interactive Demographic Analysis System (IDEAS), website, June 3, 2010. As of June 22, 2010:
http://w11.afpc.randolph.af.mil/vbin/broker8.exe?_program=ideas.IDEAS_Default.sas&_service=prod2pool3&_debug=0

Armed Forces Crossroads, website, 2010. As of October 7, 2010:
http://www.afcrossroads.com/

Albano, Sondra, *Barriers and Facilitators to Use of Air Force Family Support Centers (FSCs): Lessons for Civilian and Military Sectors*, Ann Arbor, Mich.: UMI, 1997.

Albano, Sondra, "What Society Learned from the U.S. Military's System of Family Support," *National Council on Family Relations Report*, Vol. 47, No. 1, 2002, pp. F6–F8.

American Association for Public Opinion Research, *Standard Definitions: Final Dispositions of Case Codes and Outcome Rates for Surveys*, Deerfield, Ill.: Author, 2009.

Bell, Bruce, Joel M. Teitelbaum, and Walter R. Schumm, "Keeping the Home Fires Burning: Family Support Issues," *Military Review*, March–April 1996, pp. 80–84.

Blumberg, Stephen J., and Julian V. Luke, *Wireless Substitution: Early Release of Estimates from the National Health Interview Survey, January–June 2007*, Hyattsville, Md.: National Center for Health Statistics, 2007.

Booth, Bradford, "Contextual Effects of Military Presence on Women's Earnings," *Armed Forces & Society*, Vol. 30, No. 1: 2003, pp. 25–52.

Booth, Bradford, Mady Wechsler Segal, and D. Bruce Bell, *What We Know About Army Families: 2007 Update*, Fairfax, Va.: ICF International, 2007.

Bourg, Chris, and Mady Wechsler Segal, "The Impact of Family Supportive Policies and Practices on Organizational Commitment to the Army," *Armed Forces & Society*, Vol. 25, No. 4, Summer 1999, pp. 633–652.

Bowen, Gary L., and Dennis K. Orthner, "Single Parents in the U.S. Air Force," *Family Relations*, Vol. 35, 1986, pp. 45–52.

Burrell, Lolita M., Gary A. Adams, Doris Briley Durand, and Carl Andrew Castro, "The Impact of Military Lifestyle Demands on Well-Being, Army, and Family Outcomes," *Armed Forces & Society*, Vol. 33, No. 1, October 2006, pp. 43–58.

Burrell, Lolita, Doris Durand, and Jennifer Fortado, "Military Community Integration and Its Effect on Well-Being and Retention," *Armed Forces & Society*, Vol. 30, No. 1, Fall 2003, pp. 7–24.

Carden, Army Sgt. 1st Class Michael J., "Law Gives Military Renters More Protection Against Foreclosures," American Forces Press Service, June 11, 2009. As of June 30, 2010:
http://www.af.mil/news/story.asp?id=123153787

Carlsmith, Lyn, "Effect of Early Father Absence on Scholastic Aptitude," *Harvard Educational Review*, Vol. 34, No. 1, 1964, pp. 3–21.

Carrol, Joseph, "Most Americans 'Very Satisfied' with Their Personal Lives," Princeton, N.J.: Gallup website, December 31, 2007. As of June 29, 2010:
http://www.gallup.com/poll/103483/most-americans-very-satisfied-their-personal-lives.aspx

Castaneda, Laura Werber, and Margaret C. Harrell, "Military Spouse Employment: A Grounded Theory Approach to Experiences and Perceptions, *Armed Forces & Society*, Vol. 34, No. 3, 2008, pp. 389–412.

Castaneda, Laura Werber, Margaret C. Harrell, Danielle M. Varda, Kimberly Curry Hall, Megan K. Beckett, and Stefanie Stern, *Deployment Experiences of Guard and Reserve Families: Implications for Support and Retention*, Santa Monica, Calif.: RAND Corporation, MG-645-OSD, 2008. As of September 23, 2010:
http://www.rand.org/pubs/monographs/MG645/

Chandra, Anita, Lisa Jaycox, Terri L. Tanielian, Rachel M. Burns, Teague Ruder, and Bing Han, "Children on the Homefront: The Experiences of Children from Military Families," *Pediatrics*, Vol. 125, No. 1, January 2010, pp. 16–25.

Chandra, Anita, Rachel M. Burns, Terri Tanielian, Lisa H. Jaycox, "Understanding the Deployment Experience for Children from Military Families," in Shelley MacDermid Wadsworth and David Riggs, eds., *U.S. Military Families Under Stress*, New York: Springer, forthcoming.

Chandra, Anita, Stacy Ann Hawkins, Amy Richardson, "The Impact of Parental Deployment on Child Social and Emotional Functioning: Perspectives of School Staff, *Journal of Adolescent Health*, Vol. 146, No. 3, 2010, pp. 218–223.

Cooke, Thomas J., and Karen Speirs, "Migration and Employment Among The Civilian Spouses of Military Personnel," *Social Science Quarterly*, Vol. 86, No. 2, 2005, pp. 343–355.

Cooney, Richard, Mady W. Segal, and Karin De Angelis, "Moving With the Military: Race, Class, and Gender Differences in the Employment Consequences of Tied Migration," paper presented at the American Sociological Association meetings, San Francisco, Calif., August 10, 2009.

Cozza, Stephen J., Ryo S. Chun, and James A. Polo, "Military families and children during operation Iraqi Freedom," *Psychiatric Quarterly*, Vol. 76, No. 4, 2005, pp. 371–378.

Craft & Hobby Association, "Crafting Remains Strong During the Recession," news release, Elmwood Park, N.J.: April 27, 2010. As of June 24, 2010:
http://www.craftandhobby.org/cgi-bin/pressrelease.cgi?func=ShowRelease&releaseid=335

Defense Department Advisory Committee on Women in the Services, *2005 Report*, Washington, D.C., 2005.

Defense Manpower Data Center, *2006 Survey of Active-Duty Spouses: Administration, Datasets and Codebook*, Arlington, Va., 2007.

———, *August 2009 Status of Forces Survey of Active-Duty Members: Tabulations of Responses*, Arlington, Va., 2010.

DMDC—*See* Defense Manpower Data Center.

DoD—*See* U.S. Department of Defense.

Donley, Michael B., "The Year of the Air Force Family," remarks to the Air Force Sergeants Association, August 19, 2000. As of November 7, 2009:
http://www.af.mil/information/speeches/speech.asp?id=497

Drummet, Amy Reinkober, Marilyn Coleman, and Susan Cable, "Military Families Under Stress: Implications for Family Life Education," *Family Relations*, Vol. 52, No. 3, 2004, pp. 279–280.

Ender, Morten G., Kathleen Campbell, Toya Davis, and Patrick Michaelis, "Greedy Media: Army Families, Embedded Reporting, and the War in Iraq," *Sociological Focus*, Vol. 40, No. 1, 2007, pp. 48–71.

Finney, Michael, "Foreclosure Crisis Hits Military Family," *ABC Local*, April, 12, 2010. As of June 30, 2010:
http://abclocal.go.com/kgo/story?section=news/7_on_your_side&id=7382297

Flake, Eric, Beth Ellen Davis, Patti L. Johnson, and Laura S. Middleton, "The Psychosocial Effects of Deployment on Military Children," *Journal of Developmental and Behavioral Pediatrics*, Vol. 30, No. 4, 2009, pp. 271–278.

Harrell, Margaret C., Nelson Lim, Laura Werber Castaneda, and Daniella Golinelli, *Working Around the Military: Challenges to Military Spouse Employment and Education,* Santa Monica, Calif.: RAND Corporation, MG-196-OSD, 2004. As of September 23, 2010:
http://www.rand.org/pubs/monographs/MG196/

Harrell, Margaret C., *Invisible Women: Junior Enlisted Army Wives*, Santa Monica, Calif.: RAND Corporation, MG-1223, 2000. As of September 23, 2010:
http://www.rand.org/pubs/monograph_reports/MR1223/

Hodge, Isabel, "Establishing a Support Group for Military Families with Special Needs," *Exceptional Parent*, Vol. 37, No. 6, June 2007, pp. 86–88.

Hoge, C. W., C. A. Castro, S. C. Messer, D. McGurk, D. I. Cotting, and R. L. Koffman, "Combat Duty In Iraq And Afghanistan, Mental Health Problems, And Barriers To Care," *New England Journal of Medicine*, Vol. 351, No. 1, July 2004, pp. 13–22.

Hosek, James R., Jennifer Kavanagh, and Laura Miller, *How Deployments Affect Service Members,* Santa Monica, Calif.: RAND Corporation, MG-432-RC, 2006. As of September 23, 2010:
http://www.rand.org/pubs/monographs/MG432/

Hoshmand, Lisa Tsoi, and Andrea L. Hoshmand, "Support for Military Families and Communities," *Journal of Community Psychology*, Vol. 35, No. 2, 2007, pp. 171–180.

Howley, Kathleen M., "Foreclosures in Military Towns Surge at Four Times U.S. Rate," *Bloomberg*, May, 27, 2008. As of June 30, 2010:
http://www.bloomberg.com/apps/news?pid=newsarchive&refer=home&sid=awj2TMDLnwsU#

Huebner, Angela J., and Jay A. Mancini, *Adjustments Among Adolescents in Military Families When a Parent Is Deployed*, Lafayette, Ind.: Purdue University, 2005.

Jensen, P. S., and Jon Shaw, "The Effects of War and Parental Deployment Upon Children and Adolescents," in R. J. Ursano and A. E. Norwood, eds., *Emotional Aftermath of the Persian Gulf War: Veterans, Families, Communities, and Nations*, Washington, D.C.: American Psychiatric Press, 1996.

Lavrakas, Paul J., Charles D. Shuttles, Charlotte Steeh, and Howard Fienberg, "The State of Surveying Cell Phone Numbers in the United States: 2007 and Beyond," *Public Opinion Quarterly*, Vol. 71, No. 5, 2007, pp. 840–854.

Lazo, Alejandro, "Another Battle on the Housing Front: Stimulus Aid Set Aside to Help Military Families Avoid Foreclosure," *The Washington Post,* February 25, 2009. As of July 1, 2010:
http://www.washingtonpost.com/wp-dyn/content/article/2009/02/24/AR2009022403793.html

Lim, Nelson, and David Schulker, *Measuring Underemployment Among Military Spouses,* Santa Monica, Calif: RAND Corporation, MG-918-OSD, 2010. As of September 23, 2010:
http://www.rand.org/pubs/monographs/MG918/

Lim, Nelson, Daniela Golinelli, and Michelle Cho, *"Working Around the Military" Revisited: Spouse Employment in the 2000 Census Data*, Santa Monica, Calif.: RAND Corporation, MG-566-OSD, 2007. As of September 23, 2010:
http://www.rand.org/pubs/monographs/MG566/

Lipari, Rachel, Anna Winters, Kenneth Matos, Jason Smith, and Lindsay Rock, "Military Child Well-Being in the Face of Multiple Deployments," in Steven Carlton-Ford and Morten G. Ender, eds., *Routledge Handbook of War and Society: Iraq and Afghanistan,* New York: Routledge, 2010.

Lyle, Amaani, "Air Force Officals Launch Updated Key Spouse Program," *Inside AF.mil*, October 9, 2009. As of December 7, 2010:
http://www.af.mil/news/story.asp?id=123172166

Lyle, David S., "Using Military Deployments and Job Assignments to Estimate the Effect of Parental Absences and household Relocations on Children's Academic Achievement," *Journal of Labor Economics*, Vol. 24, No. 2, 2006, p. 32.

Marchant, K. H., and F. J. Medway, "Adjustment and Achievement Associated with Mobility in Military Families," *Psychology in the Schools*, Vol. 24, 1987, pp. 289–294.

Martin, James A., Leora N. Rosen, and Linette R. Sparacino, eds., *The Military Family: A Practice Guide for Human Service Providers.* Westport, Conn.: Praeger, 2000.

McClure, Peggy, ed., *Pathways to the Future: A Review of the Military Family Research*, Scranton, Pa.: Military Family Institute, Marywood University, 1999.

McCone, David, and Kathy O'Donnell, "Marriage and Divorce Trends for Graduates of the U.S. Air Force Academy," *Military Psychology,* Vol. 18, No. 1, 2006, pp. 61–75.

McFadyen, Jennifer M., Jennifer L. Kerpelman, and Francesca Adler-Baeder, "Examining the Impact of Workplace Supports: Work-Family Fit and Satisfaction in the U.S. Military," *Family Relations*, Vol. 54, No. 1, January 2005, pp. 131–144.

McKeen, Gina Vaccaro, *New Options Available for Accompanied Korea Tours*, Air Force Personnel Center Public Affairs, March 27, 2009. As of November 25, 2009:
http://www.7af.pacaf.af.mil/news/story.asp?id=123151084

Morten, Heather, "Unemployment Compensation for Military Spouses," National Conference of State Legislatures, January 27, 2010. As of July 30, 2010:
http://www.ncsl.org/?TabId=13331

Nord, Christine W., Shelley Perry, and Betty D. Maxfield, *Evaluation of MWR Services and Family Programs: Results from the 1992 DoD Surveys of Officers and Enlisted Personnel and Military Spouses, Final Report*, Rockville, Md.: Westat, Inc., 1997.

Norwood, A. E., C. S. Fullerton, and K. P. Hagen, "Those Left Behind: Military Families," in R. J. Ursano, and A. E. Norwood, eds., *Emotional Aftermath of the Persian Gulf War: Veterans, Families, Communities, and Nations*, Washington, D.C.: American Psychiatric Press, Inc., 1996.

Office of the Deputy Under Secretary of Defense, *A New Social Compact: A Reciprocal Partnership between the Department of Defense, Service Members, and Families*, Washington, D.C.: Military Community and Family Policy, 2002.

Orthner, Dennis K., *Families in Blue: Implications of a Study of Married and Single Parent Families in the U.S. Air Force*, Washington, D.C.: Department of the Air Force, 1980.

———, *Relocation Adjustment Among Army Civilian Spouses: Survey Report*, Arlington, Va.: U.S. Army Family and Morale, Welfare, and Recreation Command, 2002.

Orthner, Dennis K., and G. L. Bowen, *Families in Blue Phase II: Insights from Air Force Families in the Pacific*, Greensboro, N.C.: Family Development Press, 1982a.

———, "Attitudes Toward Family Enrichment and Support Programs Among Air Force Families," *Family Relations*, Vol. 31, No. 3, 1982b, pp. 415–424.

Pew Research Center, "Survey Experiment Shows Polls Face Growing Resistance, But Still Representative," April 20, 2004. As of March 3, 2010:
http://people-press.org/reports/pdf/211.pdf

Pierce, Penny F., Amiram D. Vinokour, and Catherine L. Buck, "Effects of War-Induced Maternal Separation on Children's Adjustment During the Gulf War and Two Years Later," *Journal of Applied Social Psychology,* Vol. 28, No. 14, 1998, pp. 1286–1311.

Pincus, Simon H., Robert House, Joseph Christenson, and Lawrence E. Adler, "The Emotional Cycle of Deployment: A Military Family Perspective," *U.S. Army Medical Department Journal*, Vol. 4, 2009, pp. 15–23.

Pisano, Mark C., "Implications of Deployed and Nondeployed Fathers on Seventh Graders' California Achievement Test Scores During a Military Crisis," paper presented at the annual meeting of the National Association of School Psychologists, Atlanta, Ga., 1996.

Pittman, Joe, and Gary L. Bowen, "Adolescents on the Move: Adjustment to Family Relocation," *Youth and Society*, Vol. 26, 1994, pp. 69–91.

Pittman, Joe, Jennifer Kerpelman, and Jennifer McFayden, "Internal and External Adaptation in Army Families: Lessons from Operations Desert Shield and Desert Storm," *Family Relations*, Vol. 53, No. 3, 2004, pp. 249–260.

Pomper, Kate, Helen Blank, Nancy Duff Campbell, and Karen Schulman, *Be All That We Can Be: Lessons from the Military for Improving Our Nation's Child Care System, 2004 Follow-Up,* Washington, D.C.: National Women's Law Center, 2005.

Raschmann, J. K., J. C. Patterson, and G. L. Schofield, *A Retrospective Study of Marital Discord in Pilots: The USAFSAM Experience,* Brooks Air Force Base, Tex.: School of Aerospace Medicine, 1989.

Rode, Joseph C., Michael T. Rehg, Janet P. Near, and John R. Underhill, "The Effect of Work/Family Conflict on Intention to Quit: The Mediating Roles of Job and Life Satisfaction, *Applied Research in Quality of Life,* Vol. 2, No. 2, 2007, pp. 65–82.

Rohall, D. E., Mady Wechsler Segal, and David Segal, "Examining the Importance of Organization Supports on Family Adjustment to Army life in a Period of Increasing Separation," *Journal of Political and Military Sociology,* Vol. 27, 1999, pp. 49–65.

Rosen, Leora, and Doris Briley Durand, "The Family Factor and Retention Among Married Soldiers Deployed in Operation Desert Storm," *Military Psychology,* Vol. 7, No. 4, 1995, pp. 221–234.

Rostker, Bernard D., *I Want You! The Evolution of the All-Volunteer Force,* Santa Monica, Calif.: RAND Corporation, MG-265-RC, 2006. As of September 23, 2010:
http://www.rand.org/pubs/monographs/MG265/

Ruger, William, Sven E. Wilson, and Shawn Waddoups, "Warfare and Welfare: Military Service, Combat, and Marital Dissolution," *Armed Forces & Society,* Vol. 29, No. 1,

Schwartz, General Norton A., "The Way Ahead," *CSAF's Vector,* July 4, 2010.

Segal, Mady Wechsler, "The Military and the Family as Greedy Institutions," *Armed Forces & Society,* Vol. 13, No. 1, Fall 1986, pp. 9–38.

Segal, David, and Mady Wechsler Segal, *Peacekeepers and Their Wives,* Westport, Conn.: Greenwood Press, 1993.

Smith, Tom W., "A Revised Review of Methods to Estimate the Status of Cases with Unknown Eligibility," Chicago: University of Chicago, National Opinion Research Center, September 2009.

Smith, Linda K., and Mousumi Sarkar, *Making Quality Child Care Possible: Lessons Learned From NCCRRA's Military Partnerships,* Arlington, Va.: The National Association of Child Care Resource and Referral Agencies, 2008.

Spera, Christopher, "Spouses' Ability to Cope with Deployment and Adjust to Air Force Family Demands," *Armed Forces & Society,* Vol. 35, No. 2, 2009, pp. 286–306.

StataCorp, *Stata Statistical Software: Release 10,* College Station, Tex.: StataCorp LP, 2007.

Tan, Michelle, "Some Letup Predicted for Deployment Tempo," Air Force Times, May 24, 2010. As of June 24, 2010:
http://www.airforcetimes.com/news/2010/05/airforce_deployments_052310/

Tanielian, Terri, and Lisa Jaycox, eds., *Invisible Wounds of War: Psychological and Cognitive Injuries, Their Consequences, and Services to Assist Recovery,* Santa Monica, Calif.: RAND Corporation, 2008. As of November 28, 2010:
http://www.rand.org/pubs/monographs/MG720/

U.S. Air Force, "Families of Students Using Assignment Deferment Program," news release, U.S. Air Force website, September 24, 2004. As of July 19, 2010:
http://www.af.mil/news/story.asp?storyID=123008757

U.S. Army, "Army Spouse Employment Partnership (ASEP) Program," *2010 Army Posture Statement*, August 15, 2010 . As of December 22, 2010:
https://secureweb2.hqda.pentagon.mil/vdas_armyposturestatement/2010/information_papers/Army_Spouse_Employment_Partnership_(ASEP)_Program.asp

U.S. Department of Defense, *Report on Predatory Lending Practices Directed at Members of the Armed Forces and Their Dependents,* August 9, 2006. As of September 22, 2010:
http://www.defenselink.mil/pubs/pdfs/Report_to_Congress_final.pdf

Warburton, Darren E. R., Crystal Whitney Nicol, and Shannon S. D. Bredin, "Health benefits of physical activity: The evidence," *Canadian Medical Association Journal*, Vol. 174, No. 6, 2006, pp. 801–809.

Wong, Leonard, and Stephen Gerras, *The Effects of Multiple Deployments on Army Adolescents,* Carlisle, Pa.: Strategic Studies Institute, 2010.

Wood, Suzanne, Jacquelyn Scarville, and Katharine S. Gravino, "Waiting Wives: Separation and Reunion Among Army Wives," *Armed Forces & Society*, Vol. 21, No. 2, 1995, pp. 217–236.

Yeatman, G. W., "Paternal Separation and the Military Dependent Child," *Military Medicine*, Vol. 146, No. 5, 1981, pp. 320–322.

Zellman, Gail L., Susan M. Gates, Joy S. Moini, Marika Suttorp, "Meeting Family and Military Needs Through Military Child Care," *Armed Forces & Society*, Vol. 35, No. 3, 2009, pp. 437–459.

Zoroya, Gregg, "More U.S. Troops Battle Foreclosure," *USA Today,* April, 25, 2008. As of June 30, 2010:
http://www.usatoday.com/news/military/2008-04-24-foreclosure_N.htm